DRAGONS AND CHIGGERS

Advance Reviews of *Dragons and Chiggers*

Dragons and Chiggers is an intimate, ekphrastic dialogue between father and son, spanning nearly ninety years of shared and remembered life. Through Howard S. Carman, Sr.'s evocative paintings and Howard S. Carman, Jr.'s lyrical poems, word and image speak to one another in a beautifully rendered exchange—some poems born from brushstrokes, some paintings stirred by verse, some pieces emerging independently from the well of experience. Rooted in the textures of the natural world, the meaning of home, and a gentle spiritual longing, the collection traces the deep currents of family, imagination, and time. What emerges is more than a pairing of art and poetry: it is an enduring conversation between generations, where memory becomes landscape and love becomes legacy.

> — DANITA DODSON, author of *Between Gone and Everlasting* and *The Medicine Woods*

With the precise language of a scientist and the exquisite imagery of a poet, Howard Carman, Jr., celebrates a lifetime of experiences in the beautiful collection *Dragons and Chiggers*. Perhaps his eye for detail began "within view / of boy too small to see over the dashboard" ("Dragons and Chiggers") or when, like his artist father, he discovered that "[s]carlet sings for us" ("Synesthesia"). In poems that both compliment and add layers of complexity to his father's lush paintings, Carman Jr.'s words are as "close as sap and pulse" ("Rumor") to the artwork. These poems and paintings meander among nature and faith, travel and personal history exploring the past and present as "our reflections" continue "chasing us" ("Seasons Past"). This collection of art and poetry is one to leave on the coffee table, not only to impress friends and visitors, but to revel in again and again.

> — KB BALLENTINE, author of *All the Way Through, Spirit of Wild,* and *Edge of the Echo*

Advance Reviews of *Dragons and Chiggers*

The expression "dynamic duo" may be a cliché, but Howard S. Carman, Sr., and Howard S. Carman, Jr., bring new life to the term in their collaborative work, *Dragons and Chiggers*. The paintings of Howard, Sr., and words of Howard, Jr., unite in a beautiful marriage of watercolor image and poetic expression that creates an artistic whole to bring delight to anyone who opens the book. That both men work from a rich scientific background—Howard, Sr., as an engineer, Howard, Jr., as a chemist—adds depth to their art. Each had successful and meaningful careers in their respective fields before Howard, Sr., picked up his paint brushes and Howard, Jr., picked up his pen. *Dragons and Chiggers* pairs both in tightly connected artistic expression, e.g., "Boston Harbor" as a painting of a sailboat in the harbor and as the title of the answering poem, and more loosely related art forms, e.g., the beautiful "Fall," a painting of a cabin set among autumn trees bearing orange leaves on stark black trunks and limbs, with the lovely poem "Synesthesia" in which music is the central motif. In *Dragons and Chiggers* the generations not only meet, they embrace one another in mutual love and celebration.

> — CONNIE JORDAN GREEN, author of *Nameless as the Minnows, Darwin's Breath,* and other titles

It is a rare and beautiful thing to witness art born across generations. This book stands as a testament not only to creative expression, but to relationship—to the quiet dialogue between a father and son, carried through watercolor and verse. Together their works form a quiet exchange—color answering language, experience meeting discovery. This collection is more than a collaboration; it reflects lineage, influence, and shared devotion to art. May readers find within these pages not only beauty, but connection—a reminder that creativity can bridge generations and that art, at its best, is an act of love.

> — ANNA KIMI PARKER, Artist

Also by Howard S. Carman, Jr.:

But Now I See: Rhymes and Reflections
If Saint Francis Lived in East Tennessee: An Illustrated Canticle of the Sun

Also by Howard S. Carman, Sr.:

Growing Up Carman, with Jane Carman McMahon
Thorn of Bexar by Robert Wuench and Howard Carman

This collection of paintings (Sr.) and poems (Jr.) captures nearly 90 years of memories, dreams, and visions for father and son. Both are ekphrastic: some poems written in response to paintings; some art painted in response to poems; some written and painted independently but in response to a common experience or memory.

DRAGONS AND CHIGGERS

Paintings and Poems

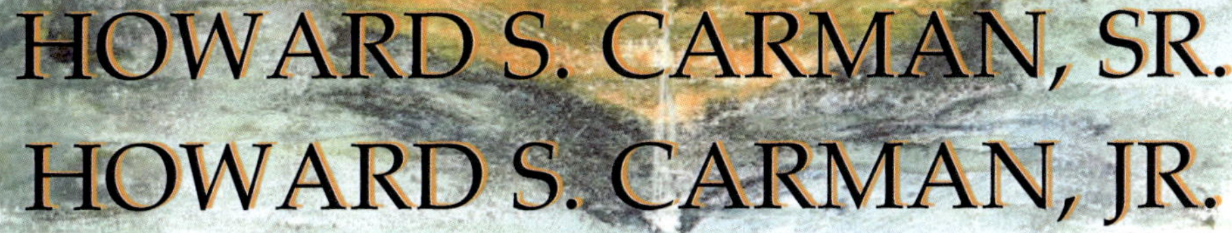

HOWARD S. CARMAN, SR.
HOWARD S. CARMAN, JR.

ISBN: 979-8-9947731-0-9 paperback
Library of Congress Control Number: 2026903075

For

Beverly and Karen
the wind in our sails

Fred and Will
our guiding North Stars

Old men ought to be explorers
Here or there does not matter
We must be still and still moving
Into another intensity
For a further union, a deeper communion . . .

—T.S. Eliot

CONTENTS

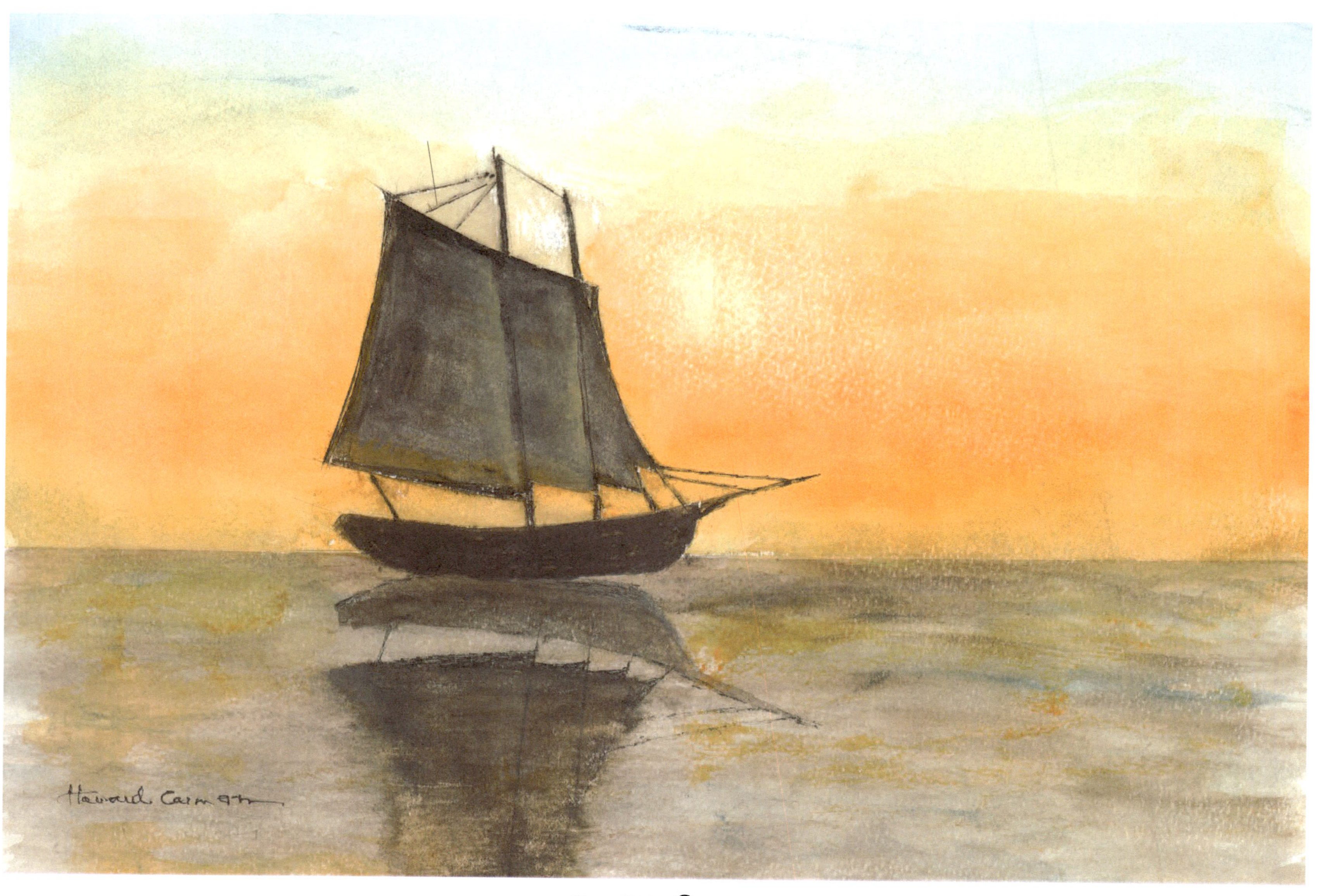

Sunset Sail

DISCOVERY

My father embarked
on his first watercolor lesson
at age seventy-two.
Now, supernovae explode
in his newborn neural galaxy.
Rays of luminous imagination
overflow into sable brushes.
Stiff but adept fingers
bring illusion toward reality.

A schooner never seen
appears in daybreak's orange,
tugged through salty mist
by lateen and gaff-rigged sails,
black hull entranced
by its twin
in a Mediterranean mirror,
like Narcissus
at a Boeotian pool.

Stars, ships, and sagas coalesce
on my quixotic quest
for a poem never written
about a ship that never sailed
until it slipped from the harbor
of my father's mind,
like Vasco da Gama
once left Lisbon.

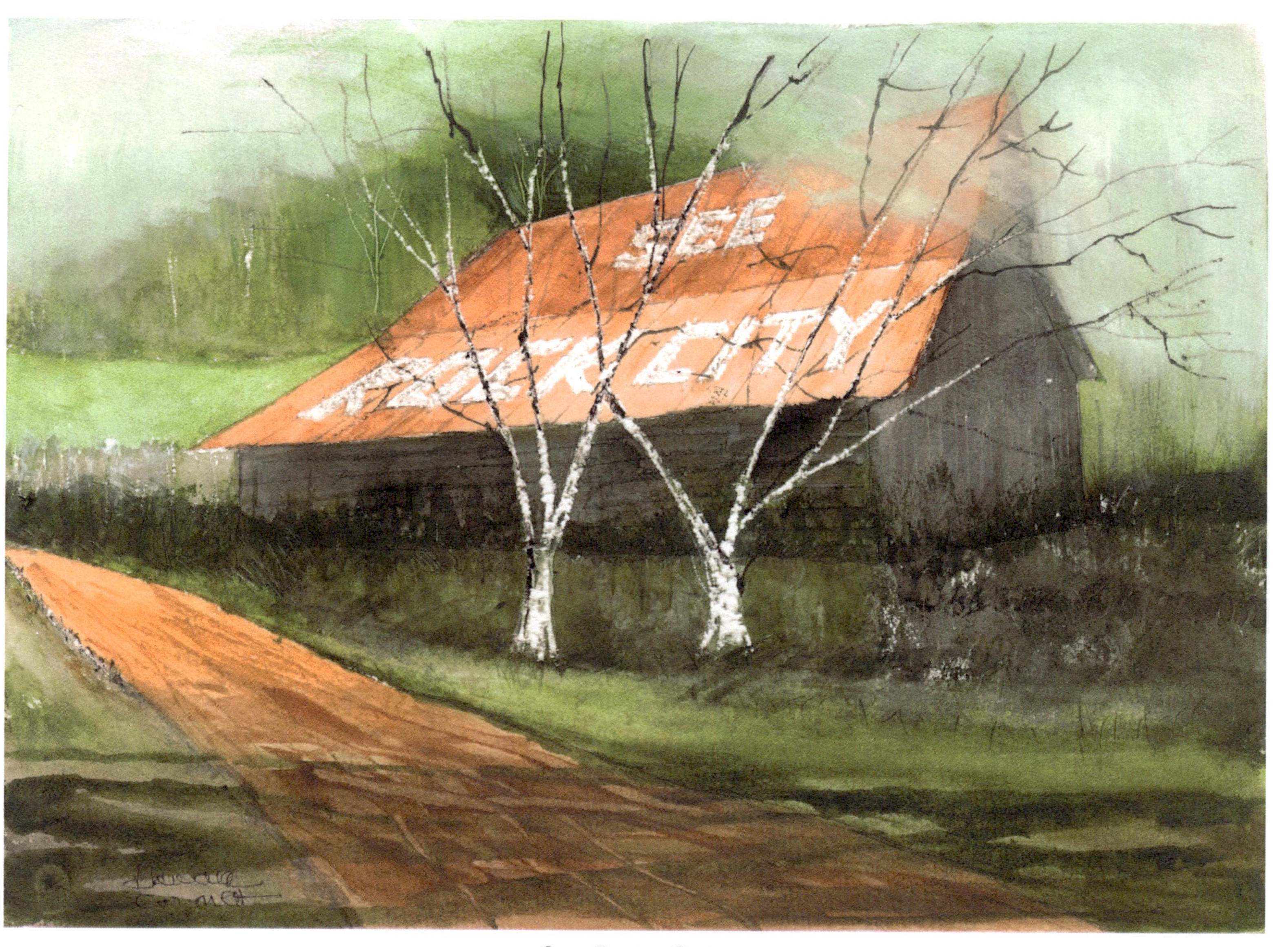

See Rock City

BARNYARD BILLBOARDS

I saw them first when I was just a kid,
about the age as when my father did.
Just off the road in Kimball, Tennessee,
white letters painted big as big could be.

My father said, *'twas there when I was born;*
it's been there since, within that field of corn.
He said that Mr. Byers painted more—
as many as nine hundred is the lore.

With four-inch brush, a ladder, and white paint,
he lettered roofs of barns without restraint.
Though most are gone, a scanty few still stand
along old southern highways once quite grand.

The See Rock City barns, to me, are dear—
each one a cherished childhood souvenir.

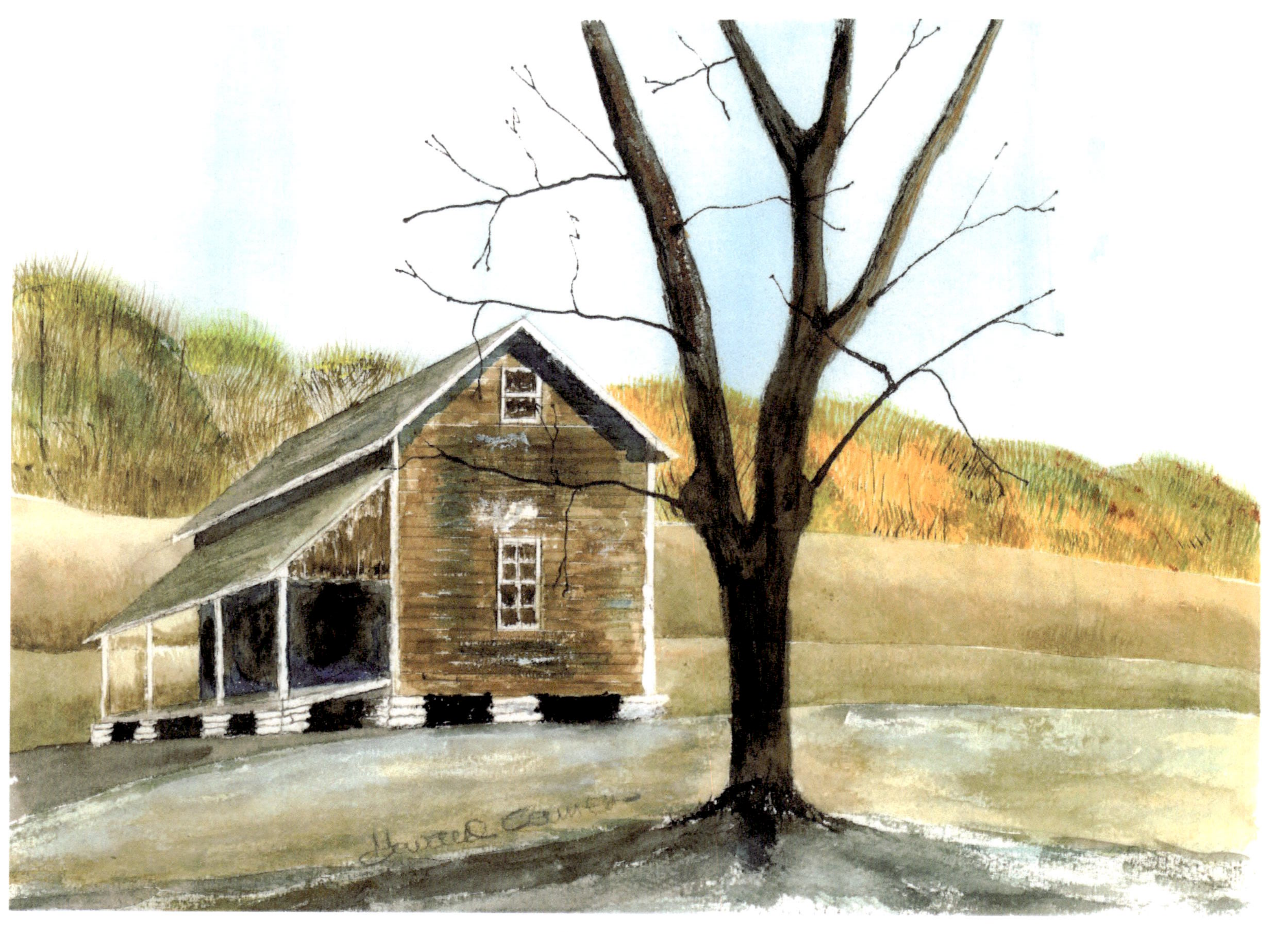

HOMESTEAD

HOMESTEAD

The tree is bare
      At the old homestead
Memories there
      Dance through my head
A rocking chair
      A feather bed
The place from where
      My childhood fled

The house was new
      Me, young and bold
Through years not few
      We've both grown old
The floor askew
      The fireplace cold
It's the house I view
      But myself behold

No longer grand
      But like the tree
We both still stand
      The house and me
Yet as it's planned
      We'll soon just be
By the painter's hand
      A memory

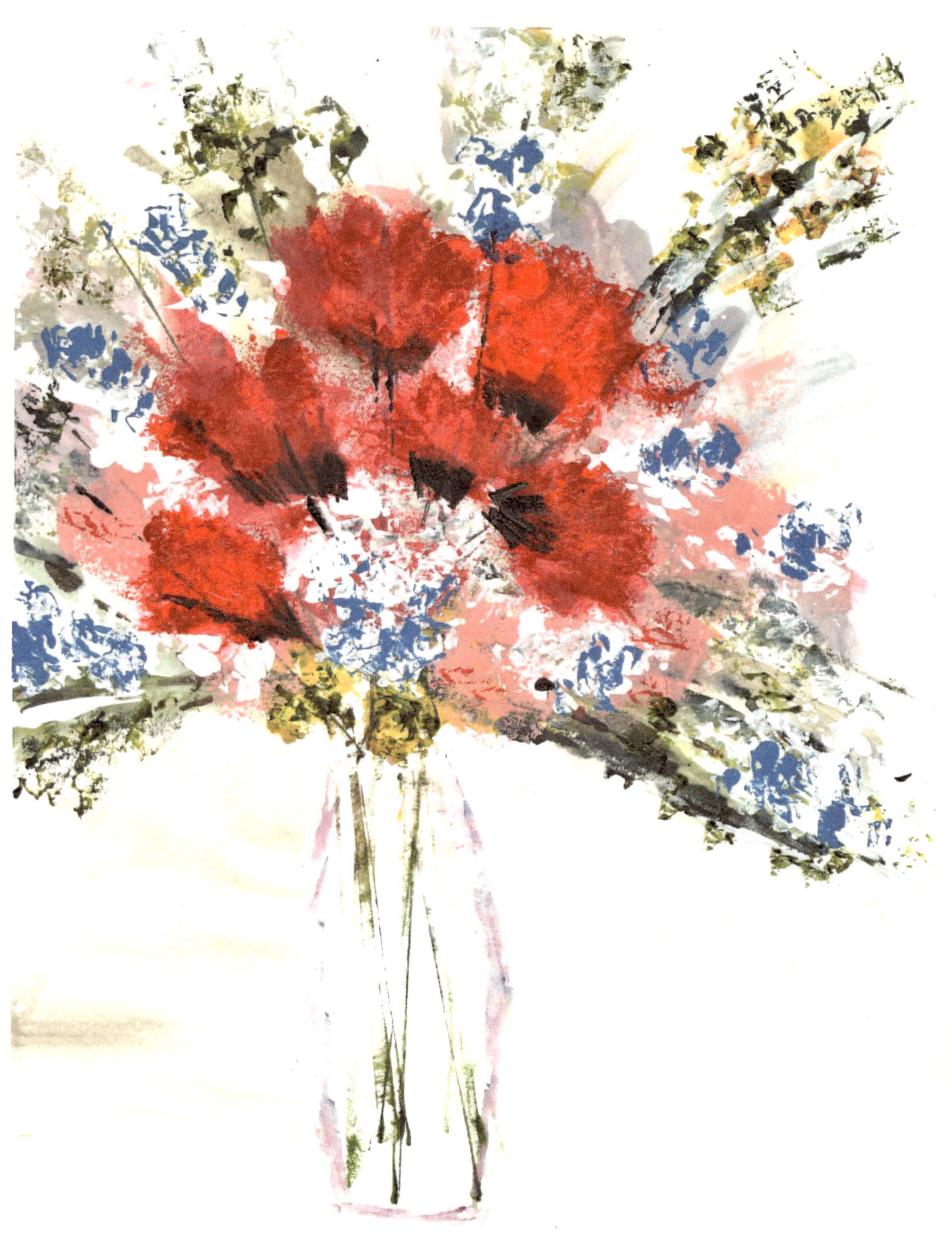

BOUQUET

REMEMBERING TOMORROWS

Last customer served,
cash register emptied and counted,
another day on her feet almost finished.

Granny locked the flower shop door,
led me down squeaky wooden steps
into a backyard filled with roses and lilies.

I was ten, she almost sixty. Across the street,
the dome of First Christian Church
swallowed afternoon sun.

Cloaked in its crescent shadow,
she began to water
weary bearded irises.

She pressed her thumb hard
against the garden hose spout
to spray those flowers farthest away.

Here, she said, *hold it like this.*
I am not sure who got wetter —
the flowers or me.

Go dry off, she laughed. *Find Gramps.*
We'll get some supper, have a good sleep,
then do it all again tomorrow.

Almost sixty, I press my thumb hard
against the garden hose spout,
teary, joyful eyes wetter than the flowers.

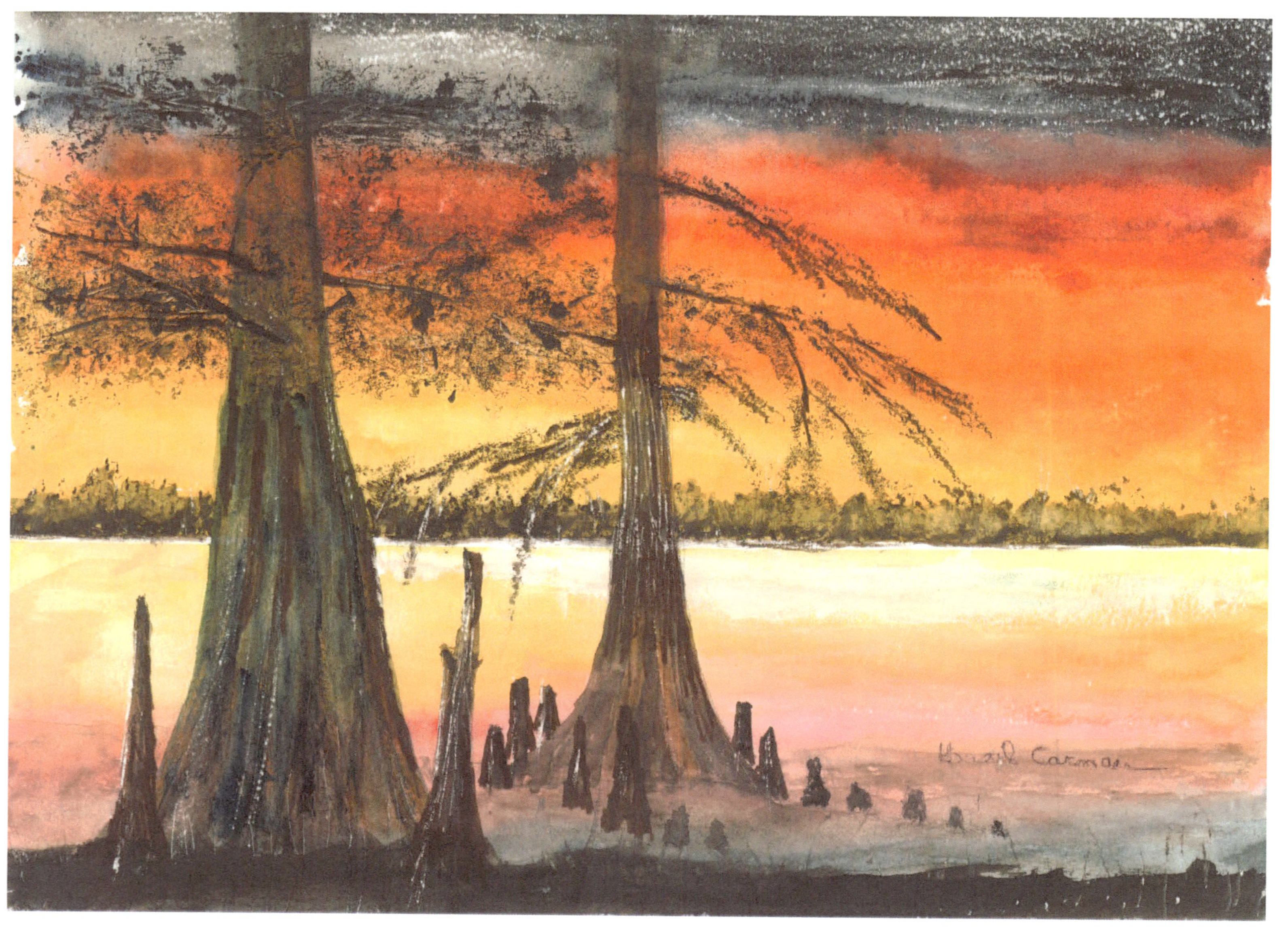

Sunset at Reelfoot

CYPRESS HORIZON

Saffron photosphere sinks
    into avocado algae bloom
that hugs bald cypress knees
    in swampy shallows.

Green, globose cones, male and female
    on each monoecious tree,
hang from slender, tassel-like branchlets,
    anxious to hatch their seeds.

Windswept wavelets prism twilight
    from Blue Basin, cast orange
and yellow like the bluegill bellies
    swimming beneath.

Legend recounts an angered Great Spirit
    who stomped and quaked the Earth, filled
his footprint with Mississippi River water
    to form this placid paradise.

My grandfather brought me here,
    just as his brought him. Someday,
like both, I will traverse the cypress horizon
    into night's final darkness.

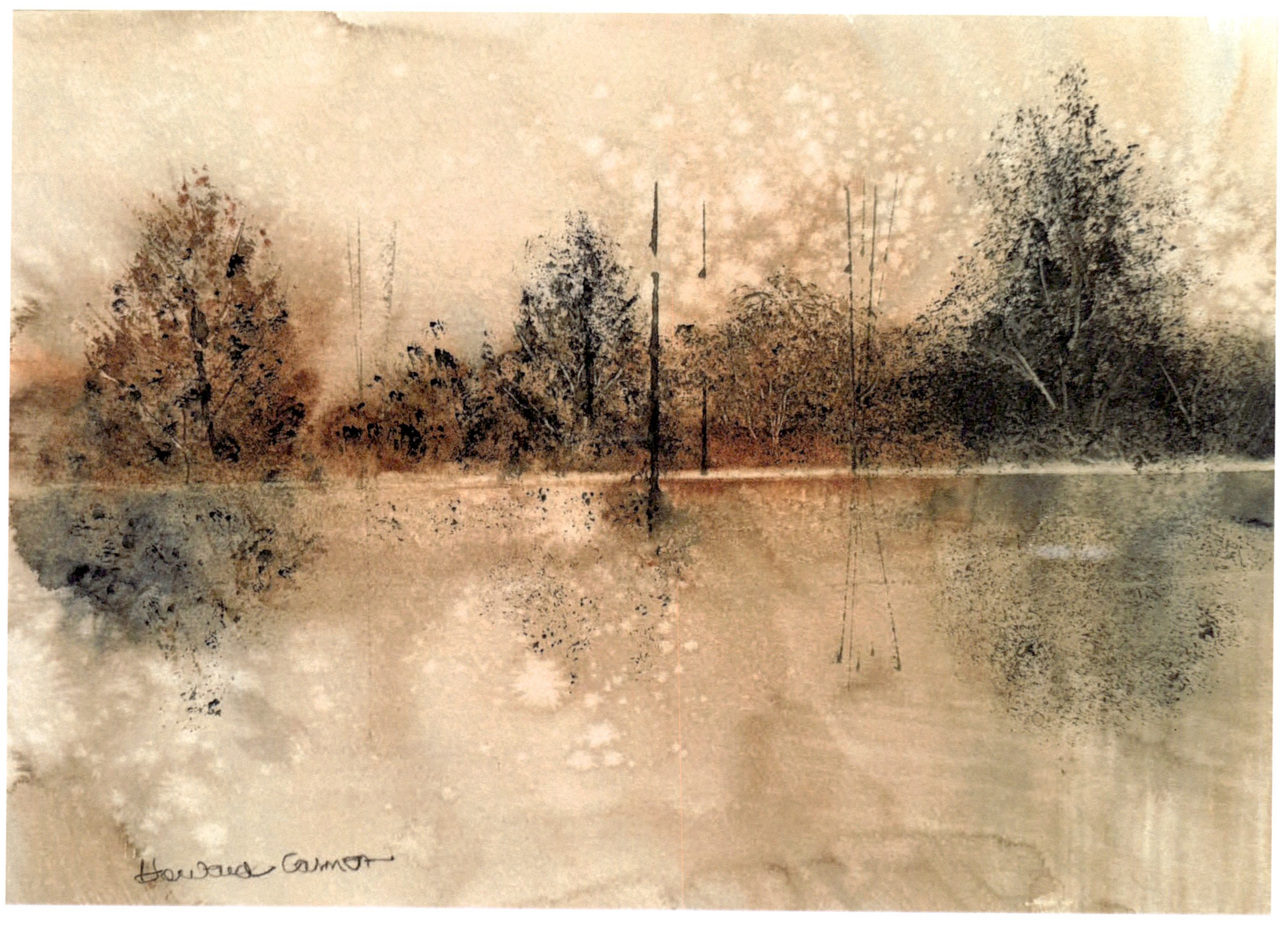

Warm Reflections

DRAGONS AND CHIGGERS

for Ernest Cotham and Josh Roberts

Crepuscular silver-spotted skippers
	skip from Ford Galaxie windshield,
leaving moth-dust dragons within view
	of boy too small to see over the dashboard.
Cornsilk-yellow station wagon trundles
	down two-rut silt and gravel to the edge
of Cecil's pond.

Wisps of morning mist too sleepy to move
	snuggle switchgrass
and broomsedge bluestem.
	GaGa hands the boy a shiny aerosol can.
Here, spray this all over you.
	Get the fabric wet. Them chiggers'll get places
you don't want got.

Denim damp, they unload poles, tackle,
	styrofoam carton of loam
loaded with nightcrawlers,
	and a cage of crickets.
Five minutes later, without warning,
	red-and-white bobber plunges with a plop.
Here, boy, I can't hold him. You reel him in.

Four hours later, stringer of forty keepers
	wriggling in the cooler, station wagon
rattles home for a feast. Today, an old man
	lifts a tumbler of Old Grand-Dad
to toast the old men who showed him
	how to slay dragons
and why some encounters
	are worth the chiggers.

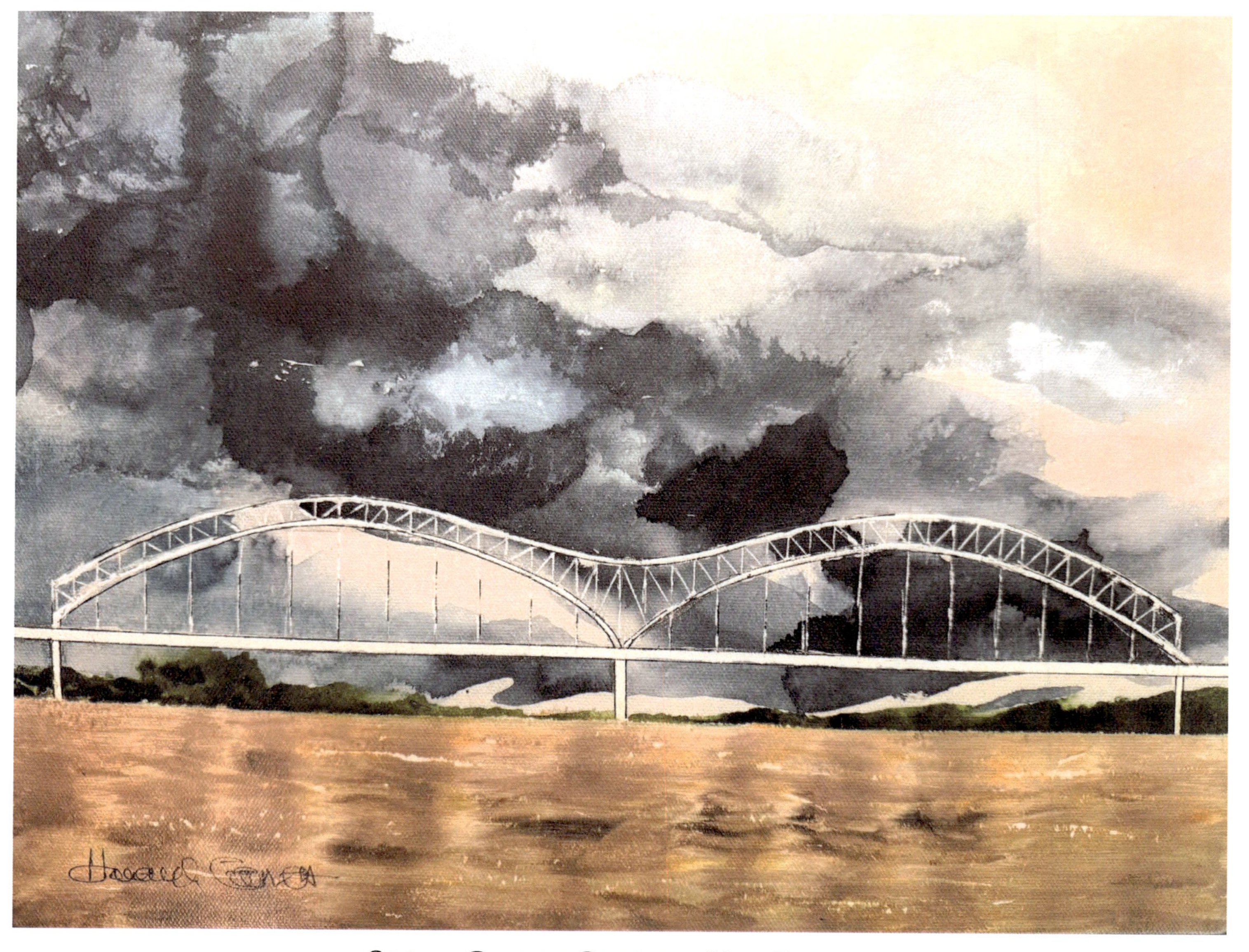

Storm Clouds Over the New Bridge

EF3 — MEMPHIS, 1970

Splinters should pierce fingertips, not bricks and bedroom
wallboards. Glass panes in wood frames, closed tight
against night at bedtime, burst inward as winds
flayed sturdy linen curtains into flimsy flags
above the bed. Brick chimney hurtled down
black-shingle roof, thuds paced with thunder
that roared and chased blue-white lightning
and half-tree silhouettes down the street.
Razer, landscaper, interior designer,
the funnel sculpted pine two-by-fours
and black oak limbs into abstract
art in driveways and living rooms.
Gone almost before it arrived,
startled neighbors gathered
among water and debris,
marveled, hugged, gave
thanks. An eleven-
year-old boy heard
distant thunder
declare, "We'll
be back." Until
he breathes
his last, he
waits.

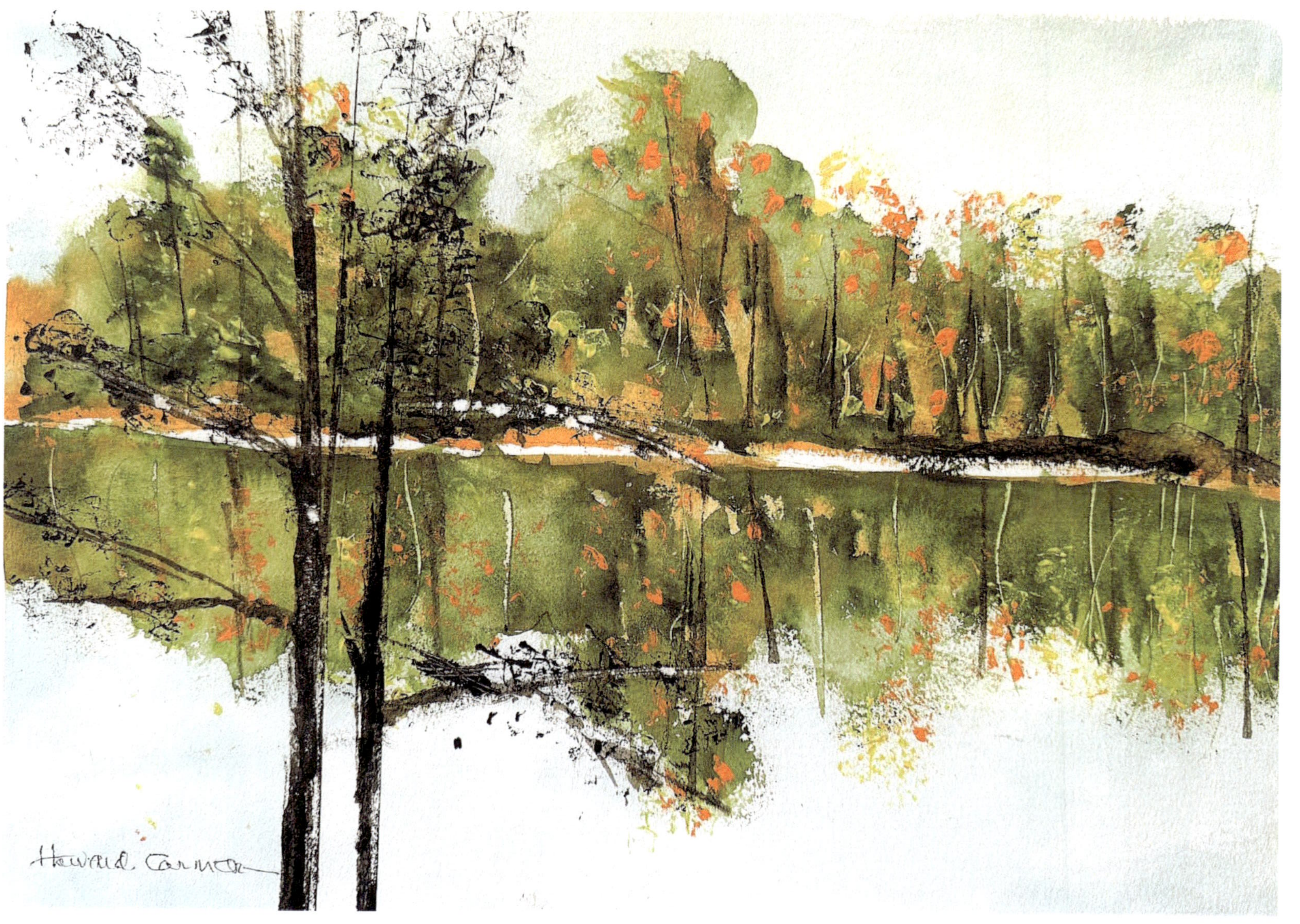

Cool Reflections

MARVEL AT THE SUNRISE

Nightshirt of darkness
slips down mountain shoulders
as ascending sun reaches
to cuddle the valley floor.
Deciduous dancers with bony arms
embrace evergreens in evening gowns
and waltz to the tempo
of a brisk morning breeze.

Granny loved to dance; Gramps did not.
But they tangoed once
on the Reelfoot Rift, planted a family tree
in Mississippi River alluvium
far from these foothills I now inhabit.
I think of them as I sip Folgers coffee
from a porcelain mug, like they did
with me, two generations ago.

I will not share coffee with my grandchildren—
our family name stops with me.
Not a deliberate decision, but immutable.
Instead of an acorn, I was a leaf,
lofted by wayward winds
to this verdant Appalachian valley.

When winter arrives and this leaf decays,
I hope young lovers will marvel at the sunrise,
sway in each other's arms, and watch the trees
dance over my dust.

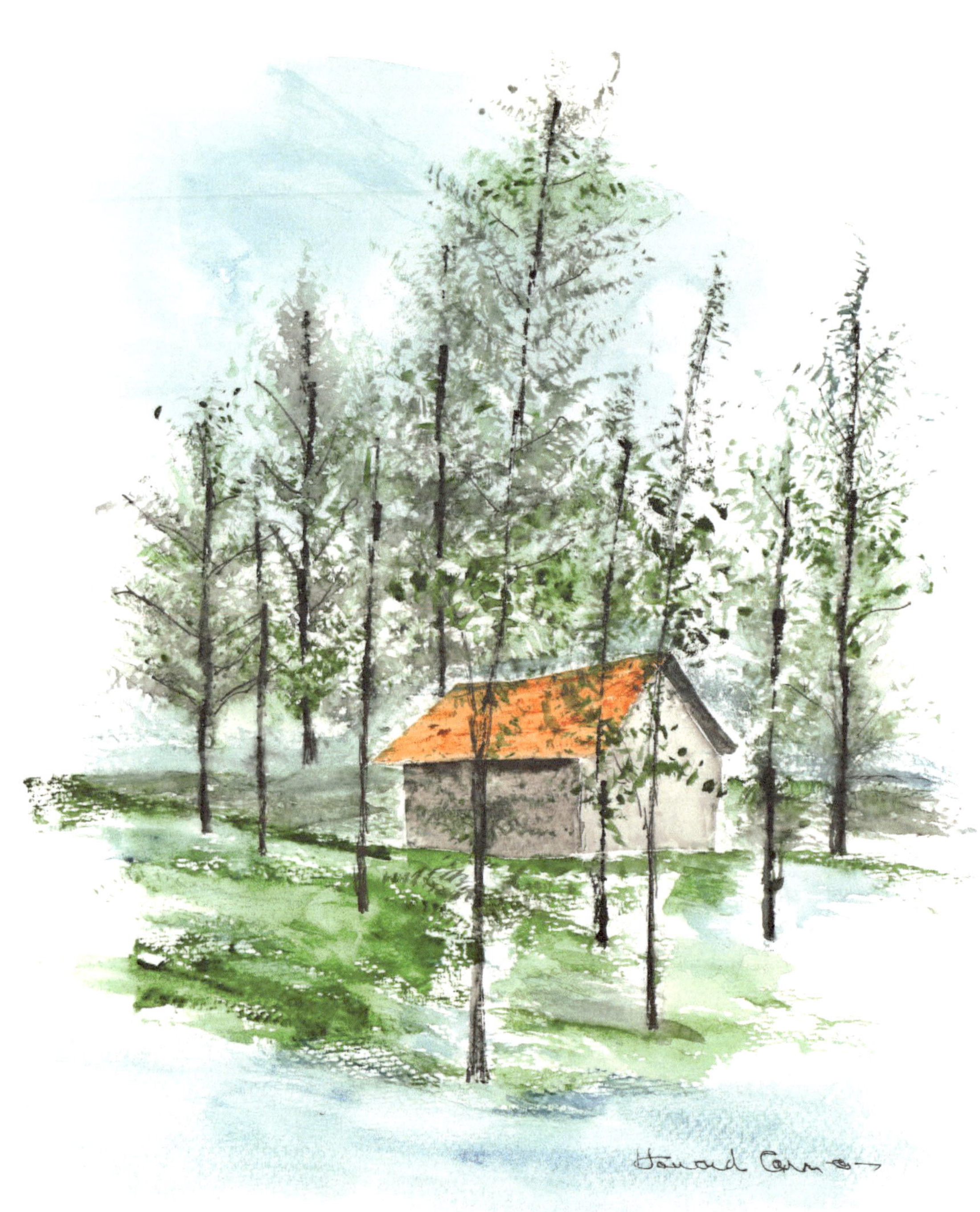

SUMMER

HOPE

after Janisse Ray

Last night in the forest
pine boughs chopped moonbeams
into musical measures
sung by a whippoorwill choir.
I nestled onto moss
beneath a quilt of summer air
embroidered with stars.

I was not alone
in my bed. Past rolled over
into a dimming horizon.
Present shuttered its eyes
to conjure a dream.
Future whispered only,
I'll see you in the morning.

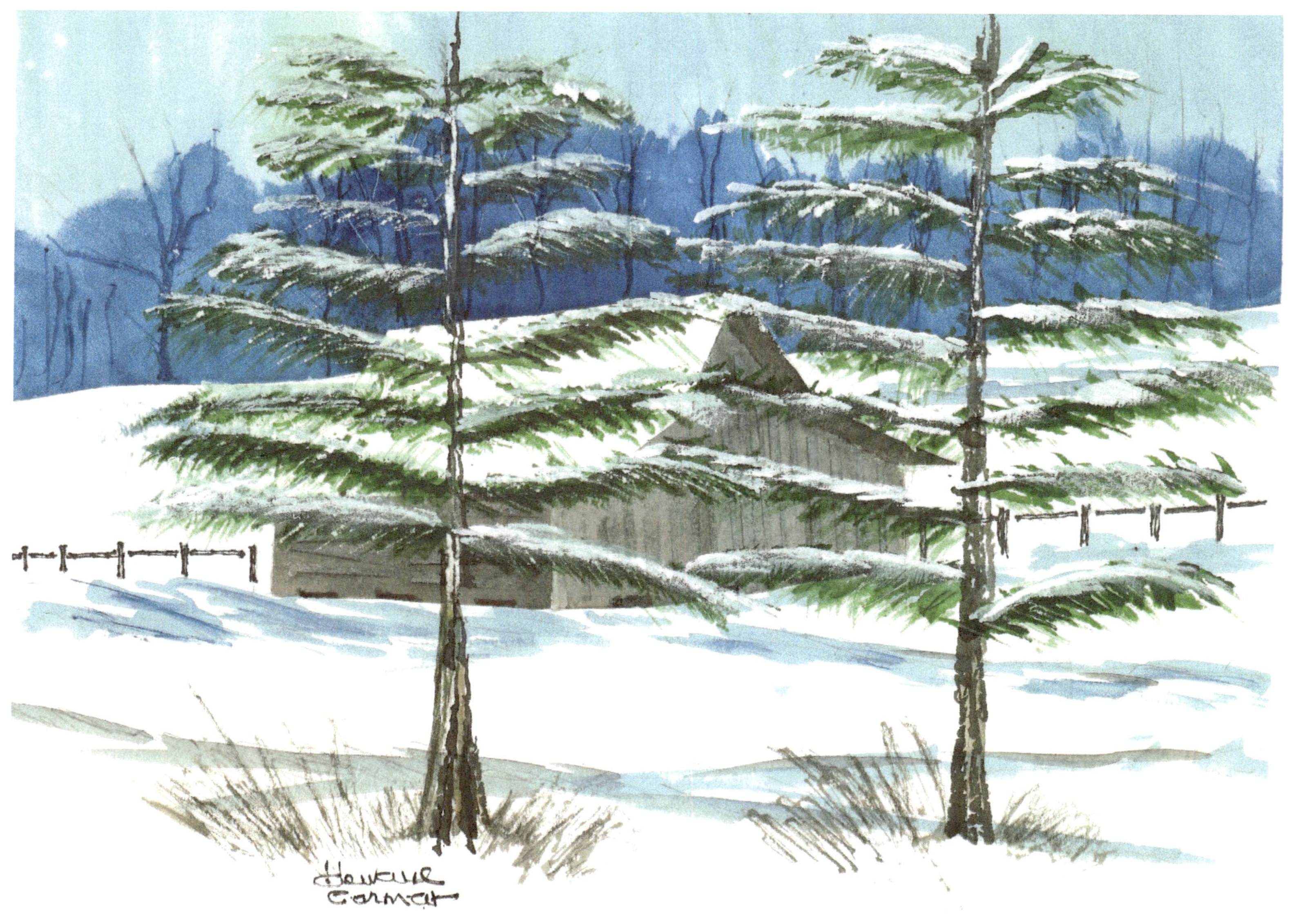

Winter Pines

BENEATH A PINE IN THE SMOKIES

Oaks stand naked
before the coming cold,
their limbs all bone and memory,
while pines keep their manners—
long green sleeves, dark tailcoats.

Wrens and tufted titmice
tuck chestnuts and elderberries
into notches and bark-creases,
secret pantries for snow-white days ahead.

The air is full of music: chirps and cheeps,
chick-a-dee-dees like plucked strings
in Sugarlands' theater.

I sit in damp moss
where we once sat together,
her shoulder against mine,
before the longest night arrived
and never entirely left.

Now the wind finds my face
the way her hand used to,
and the rock beneath me
presses its age up my spine—
older than any tree, older than bone,

old as that first dark
when the deep lay covered
and the breath of God
moved over hidden water.

Somewhere in the branches
a titmouse gives its tiny call,
and in the pause that follows
I hear her clearly:
I am home.

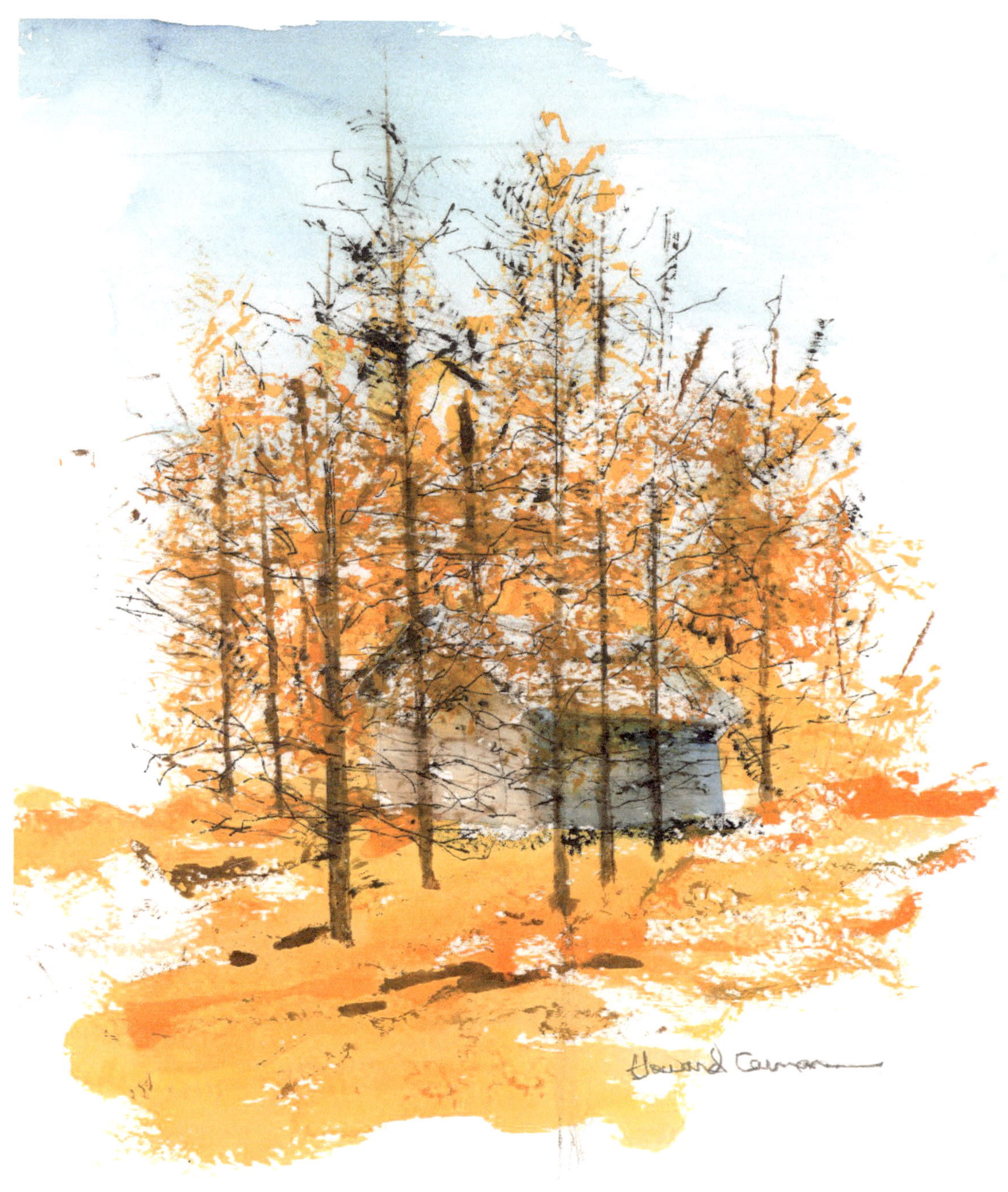

FALL

SYNESTHESIA

Scarlet sings for us,
wrapped warmly in the orange glow
of a crackling campfire.

Her voice fills the jet-black sky
and echoes among trees
whose leaves reflect hues

of her Amber Burst guitar.
We close our eyes to see
the Indigo Girls

while she plays their version
of Dylan's *Tangled Up in Blue*.
As last notes fade

into the *Purple Haze* of dawn,
someone sighs,
I wish you could see the colors.

I may be blind,
she replies,
but I do.

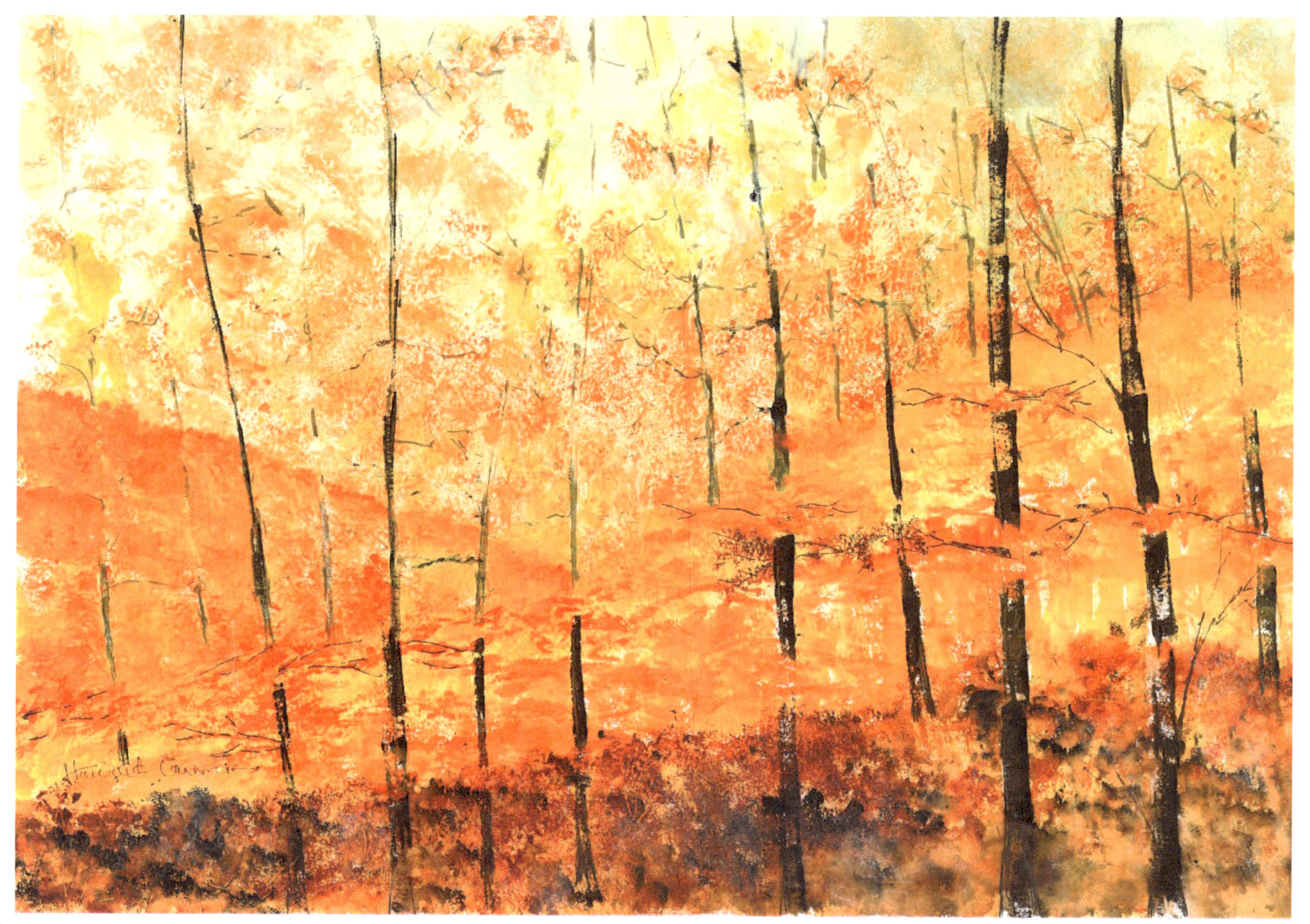

Fire in the Forest

MANN GULCH, 1949

for Wagner Dodge

Birds sense disaster, hear winds of fire,
long before orange sears the landscape.
They ascend on waving wings
past fifteen smokejumpers
who descend summer sky.

Lit by lightning in dry August heat,
cheatgrass burns like gasoline,
fueled by up- gulch winds.
Flames jump from ridge to ridge
like hares hunting clover. To flames,
smokejumpers look like fodder.

Suddenly surrounded, Foreman Dodge
lights an escape fire, beckons his crew.
But they do not hear like birds,
nor run like hares. Flames feast.
Fifteen become three.
Birds do not look back.

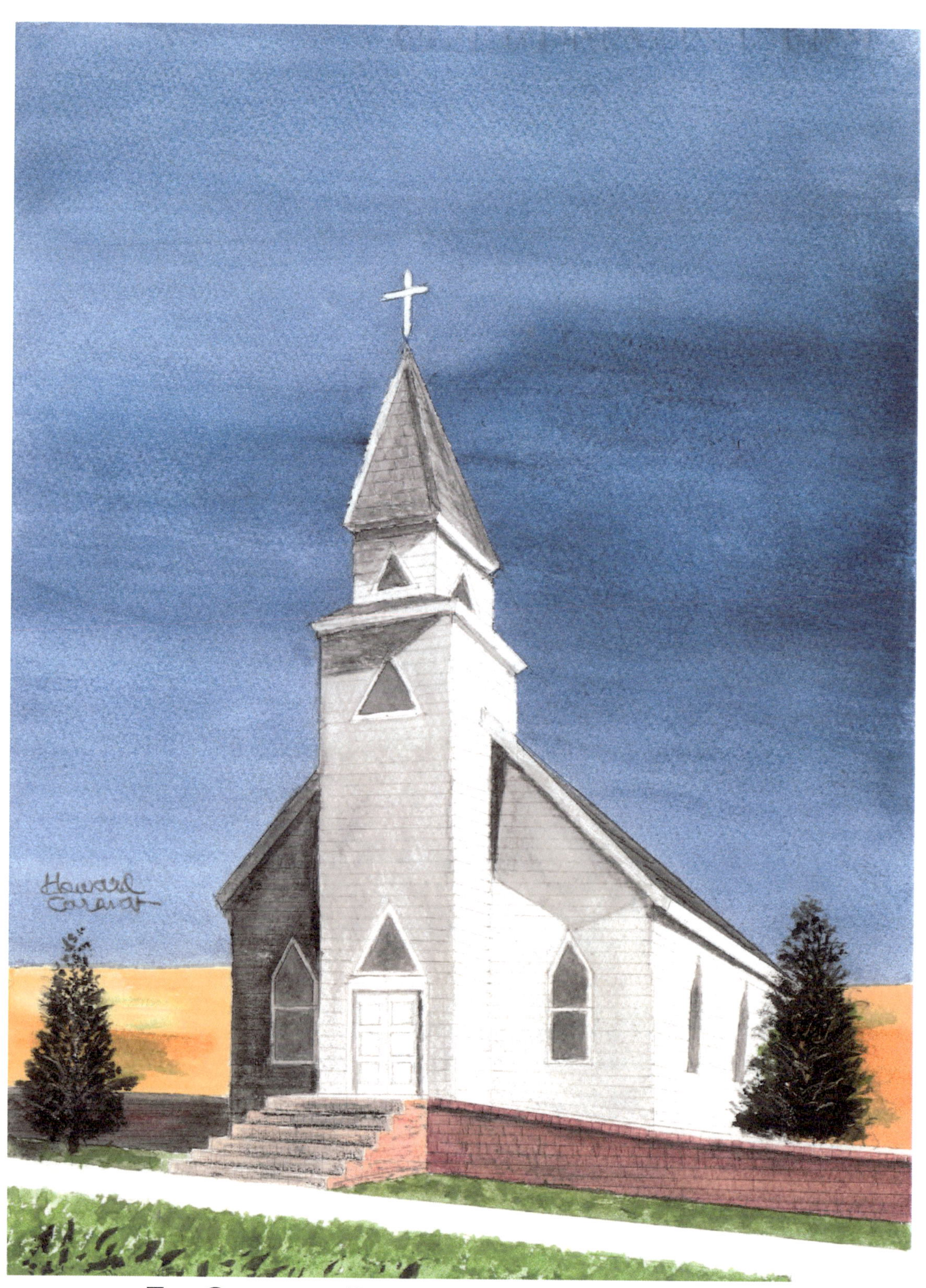

THE CHAPEL AT DISCOVERY PARK OF AMERICA

ODYSSEY

1.   *Acolyte*
I hid osseous knees and hairless arms
beneath dipped-in-blood-crimson cassock
and washed-by-the-Lamb-white surplice
to light candles for praises and mercies
from parents and pastors — sometimes God.

2.   *Youth Groupie*
I gripped my Bible like a baseball bat,
swung it in hopes of a home-run journey
to a heavenly home plate where black-vested
Head Umpire declared me safe and teammates
cheered me into our forever dugout.

3.   *Grad School Graduate*
Silenced by science, sounds of orthodoxy
disappeared like cricket chirps at first light.
Haunted by hypocrisy and haughtiness,
I dumped faith — and Bible-brandishing friends —
like rust from an old toolbox.

4.   *Midlife Mystic*
Not listening, I heard Them call; I looked
into the invisible chapel where They echoed
and saw Them — in a mirror, dimly.
Amorphous, yet palpable, like morning mist
upon my face.

5.   *Home*
Nebulous. Poignant. Profound. Personal.
Truths numerous as wildflowers: Bluebonnet,
Indian Paintbrush, Drummond Phlox,
all growing together in the field around me.
I stroll and savor the mix of many fragrances,
and trust exculpations to God.

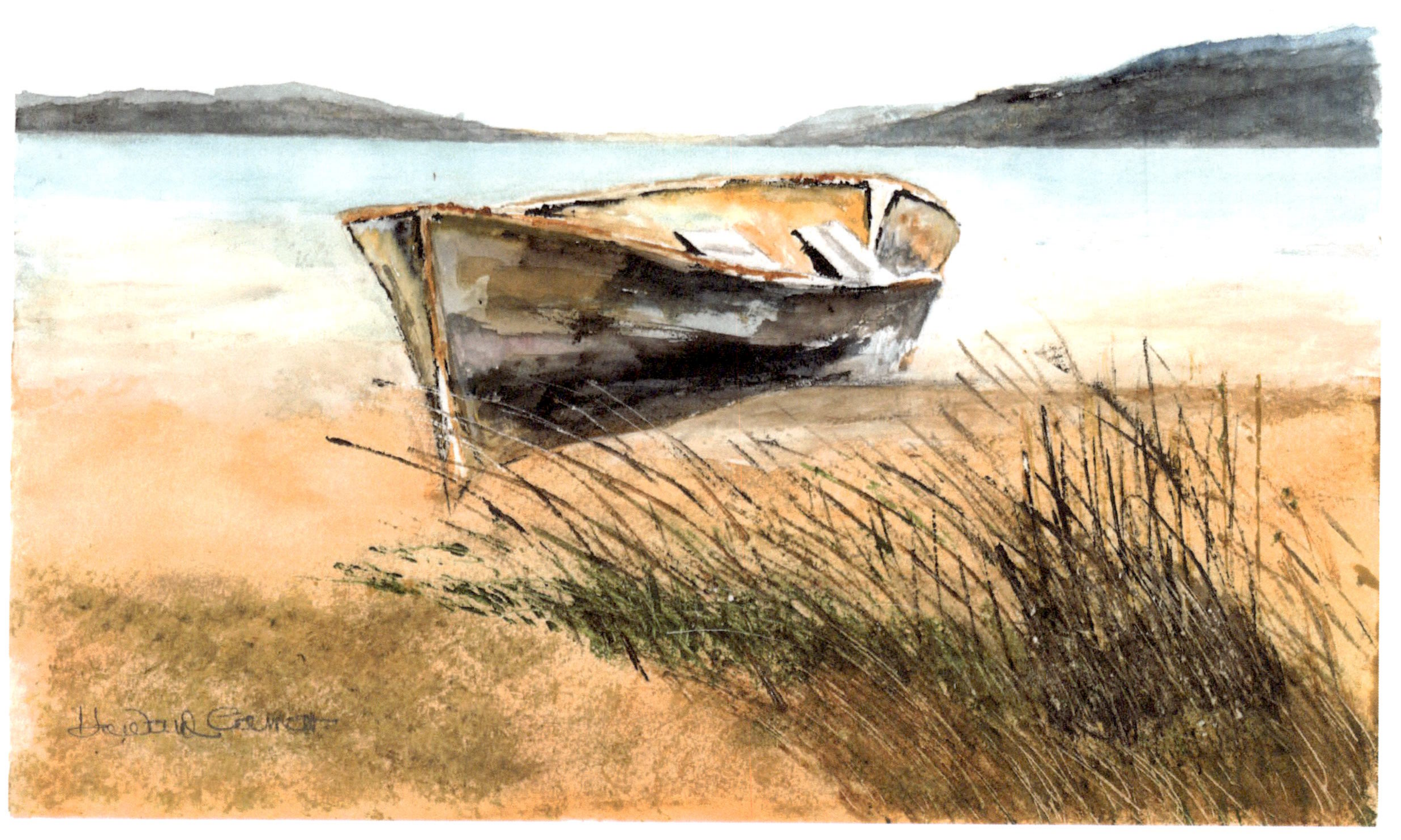

Galilee

WHO THEN WAS THIS?

Sixteen years they followed their father
daily across a sandy shore. Sweat dripped
into mortises carved in cedar and oak;
pegged planks became hulls as hammers
echoed from hawthorn and lotus
across a narrow bay where southbound
Jordan enters the Sea of Galilee.
They mended nets during day's scorch
then fished with night's shivers
beneath waves born when time began.

Three years they followed one who said,
Follow me. Left families. Walked stony paths.
Watched their friend heal the blind
with mud made from dirt and spit.
He stood in their boat and told the storm,
Be silent! Be still! and there came a dead calm.
He said to them, *I am telling you the truth,*
long before his assassin asked, *What is truth?*
Before they watched him suffocate and die.

Two thousand years have repeated their stories—
    An empty tomb.
    A friend resurrected.
    A faith others might believe what they witnessed.

And when death's storm howls at all creation,
might hear him say, as they did,
        Peace to you.
        Let us cross over to the far shore.

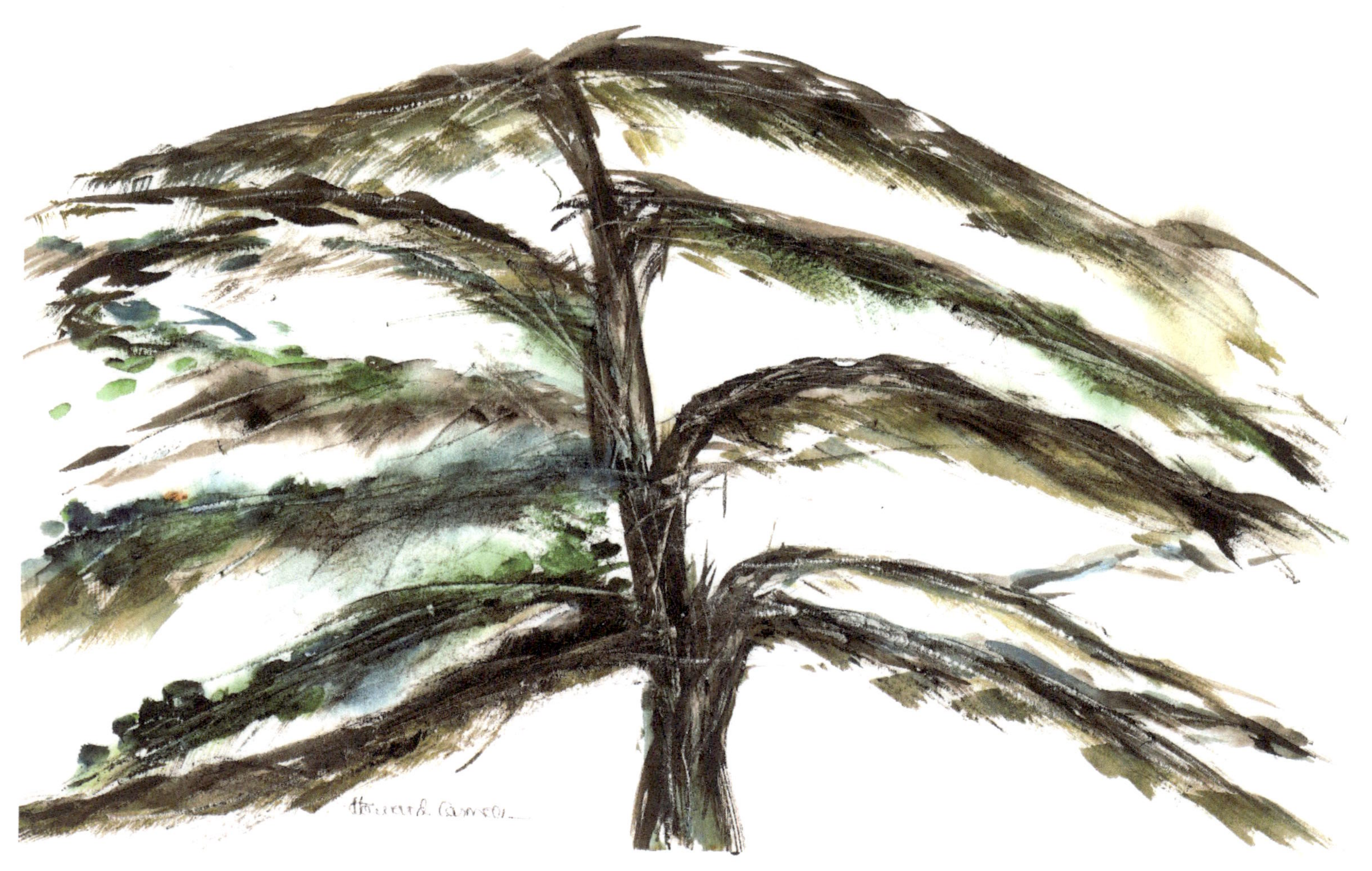

STILL IN REVISION

Before I hung lights in the dome
to separate blue day from near-black night,
I bent petiole and pedicel into hooks,
hung drupes and lanceolate curtains
of olive, avocado, and pistachio
from charcoal rods in the first windows.
My breath blurred leaves into feathers.

I wrote poetry on every bird,
quill dipped into inks of red,
yellow, blue, and violet.
Syllables stitched along a rachis
like branches to a vine,
repeating the rhythm and rhyme
of the trees.

I twisted nucleotides into words
and words into children
of countless tongues and timbres,
set them carefully in each line
to tune the harmony —
and the dissonance —
of my epic.

The first stanza
was exceedingly good.

I leave the rest
to priests —
and poets.

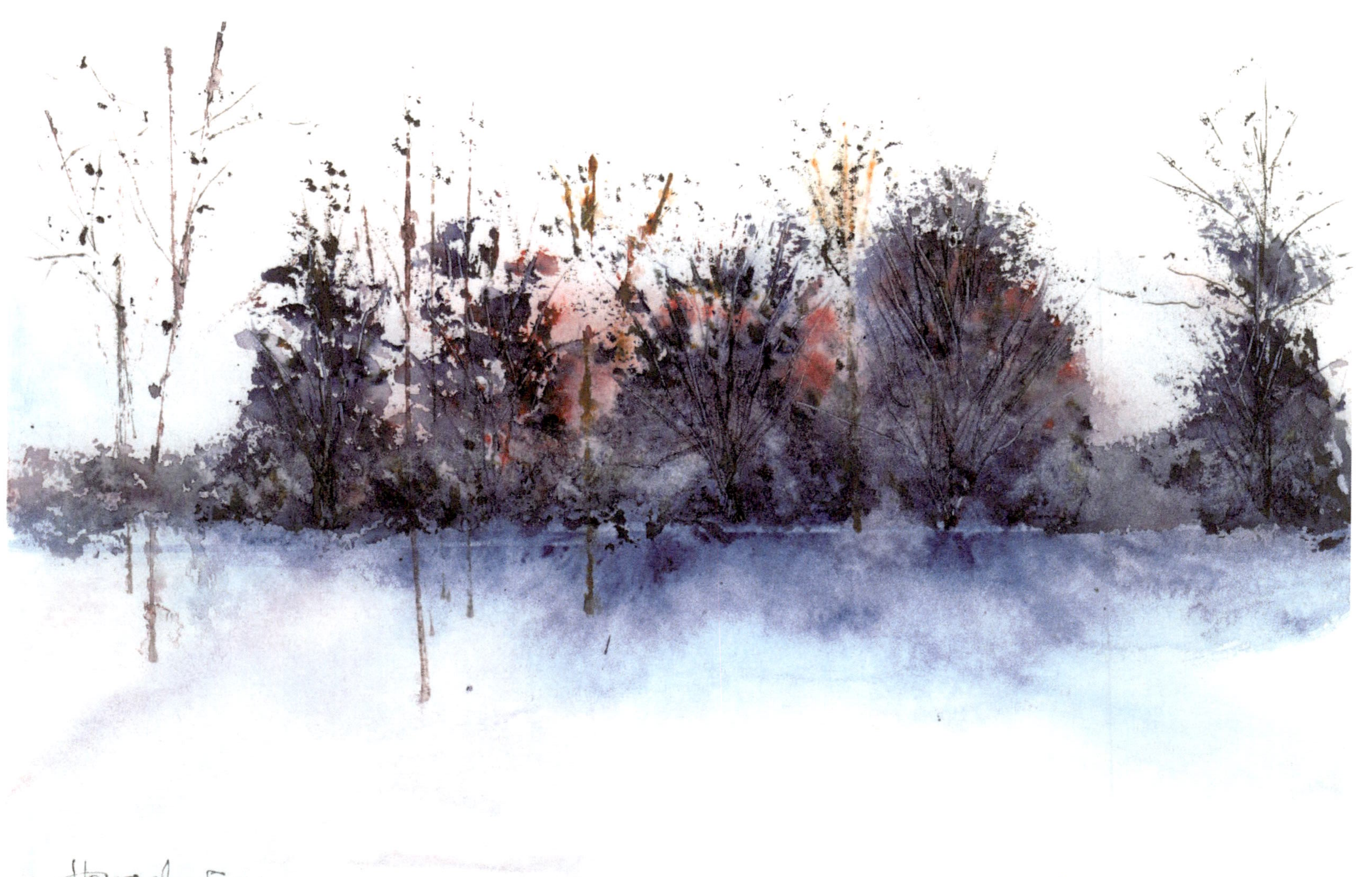

PURPLE DUSK

RUMOR

after Louise Glück

Cottonwood, maple, oak,
willow—I planted them all
for beauty,
for shade,
for my own pleasure,
for yours.

I was with you,
then within you,
close as sap and pulse.

Yet you do not love fields
with assorted flowers—
clover, violet, poppy, wild iris.
You still nail different to trees
and call it just.

And you wonder why
I do not return.

You have answered yourselves.

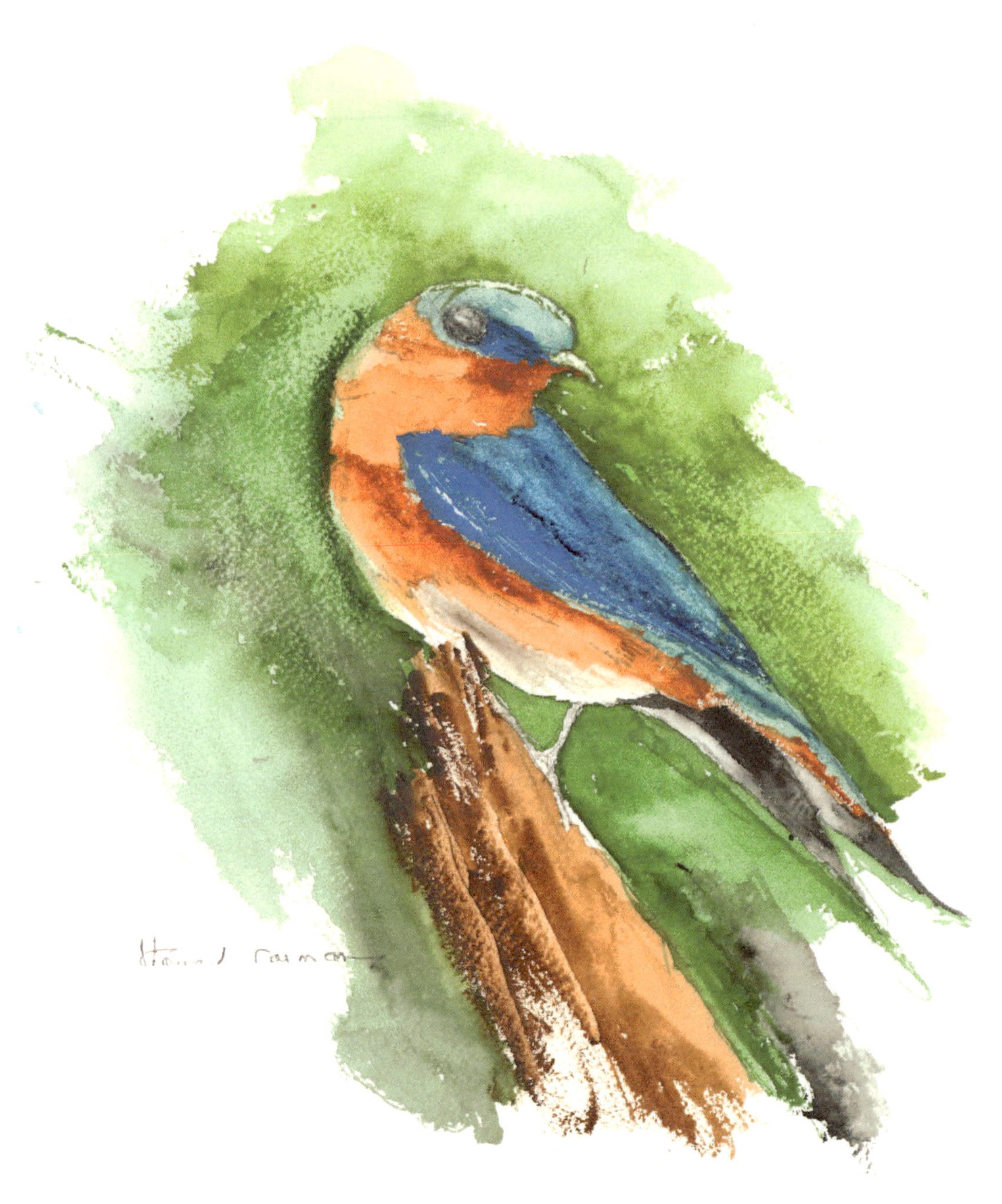

EASTERN BLUEBIRD

SITTING ON MY DECK
TALKING TO A BLUEBIRD

You perch in a pine bough
above my birdbath,
cerulean head invisible
against midday sky,
ocher breast a persimmon lost
among green needles of spring.

Plumy ailerons
guide your descent
to the basin between baskets
of canary and indigo
Johnny Jump-ups.

Sunlight detours
through a plash of prisms
as you dip, flail, and flutter
in the shallow pool. After you leave,
still water mirrors pine and cirrus.
I have no wings.

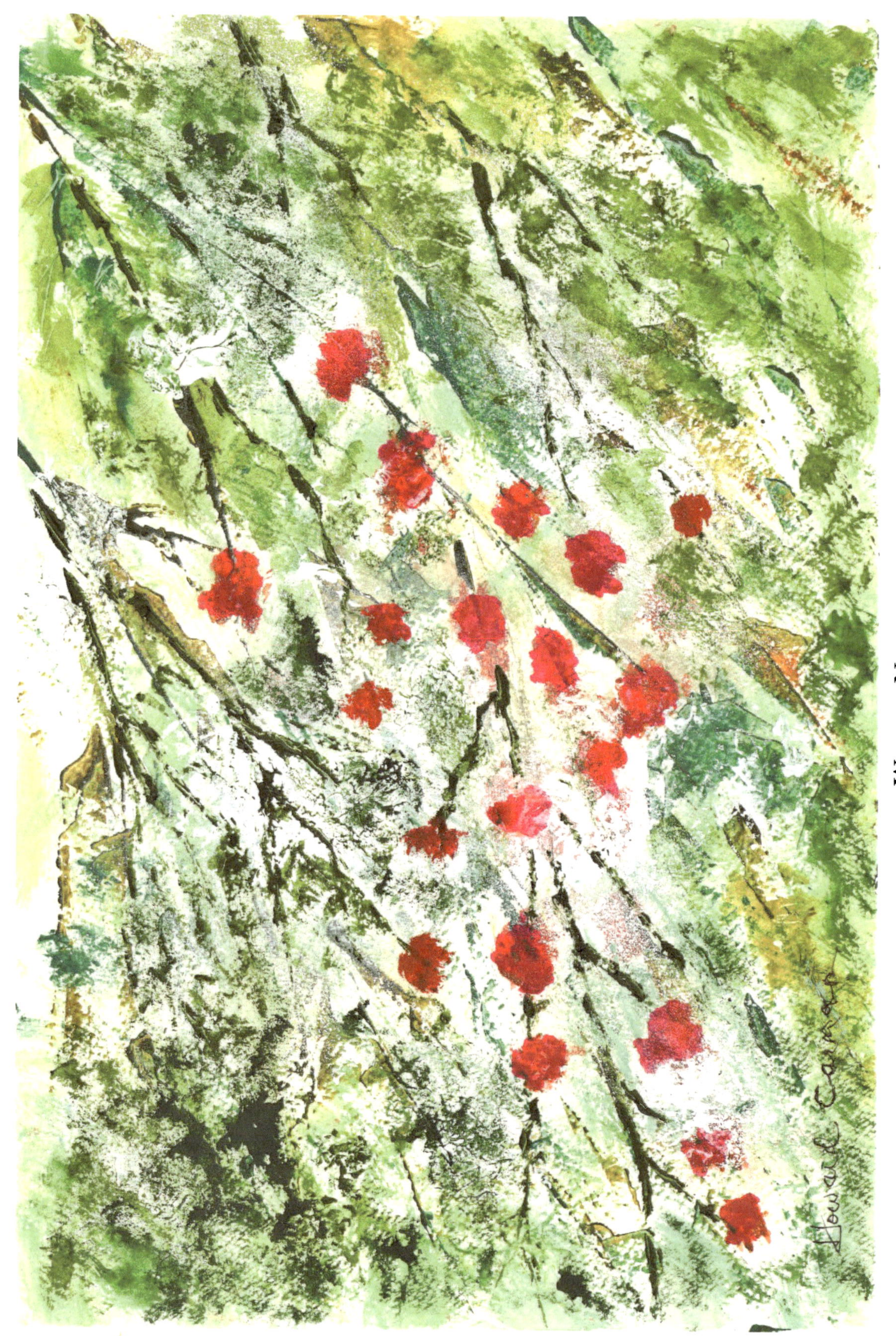

Winter Nandina

NANTEN SEASONS (南天)

Naked outside my window,
nandina berries chatter
in a southern ruby dialect
as the north wind unbuttons
their pinnate jackets.

Winter wraps white scarves
around their shoulders
and I remember spring dances—
panicles in pale prom dresses
and bright shoes—
before fall cut in, hems all aflame.

I sit with tea and lose my place
in a poetry book, as outside
they turn the page to another year.

*The Latin genus name Nandina is derived from the Japanese name nanten
(南天), which itself is derived from the Chinese name nantian zhu (南天竹),
meaning "southern heavenly bamboo."*

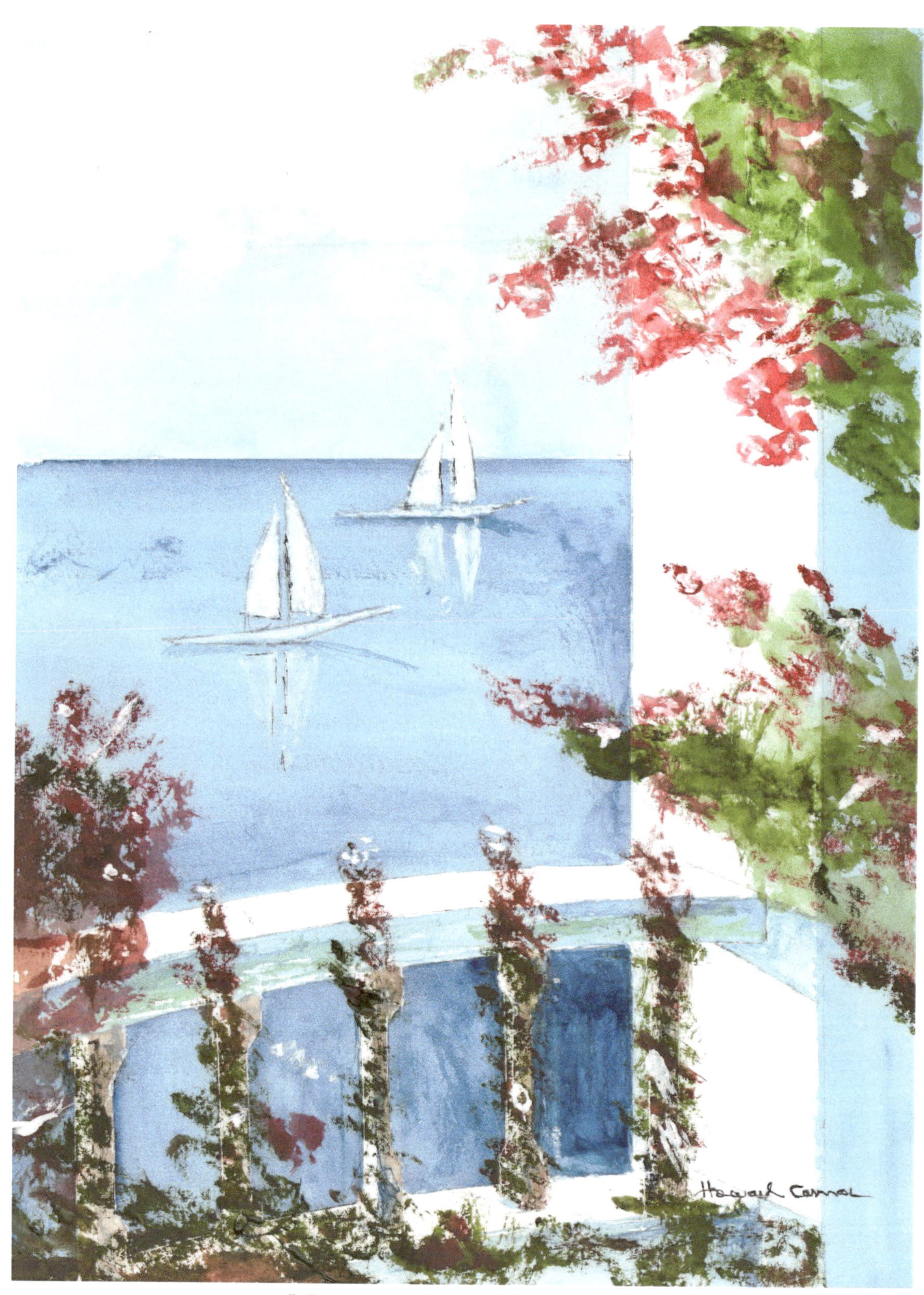

MEDITERRANEAN BALCONY

SWEET SUMMER LOVE

Clematis climbs stone columns
and opens into sunlight
along a whitewashed rail
roughened by centuries
of heat and hail
above Lago di Garda.

Perfume of vanilla, viola,
and almond rises
and hastens my pulse.

Gentle waves lift and drop
sloops with wind-ruffled sails—
quiet consonance
of hull and hemp.

I reach for your hand
and hold
what isn't there.

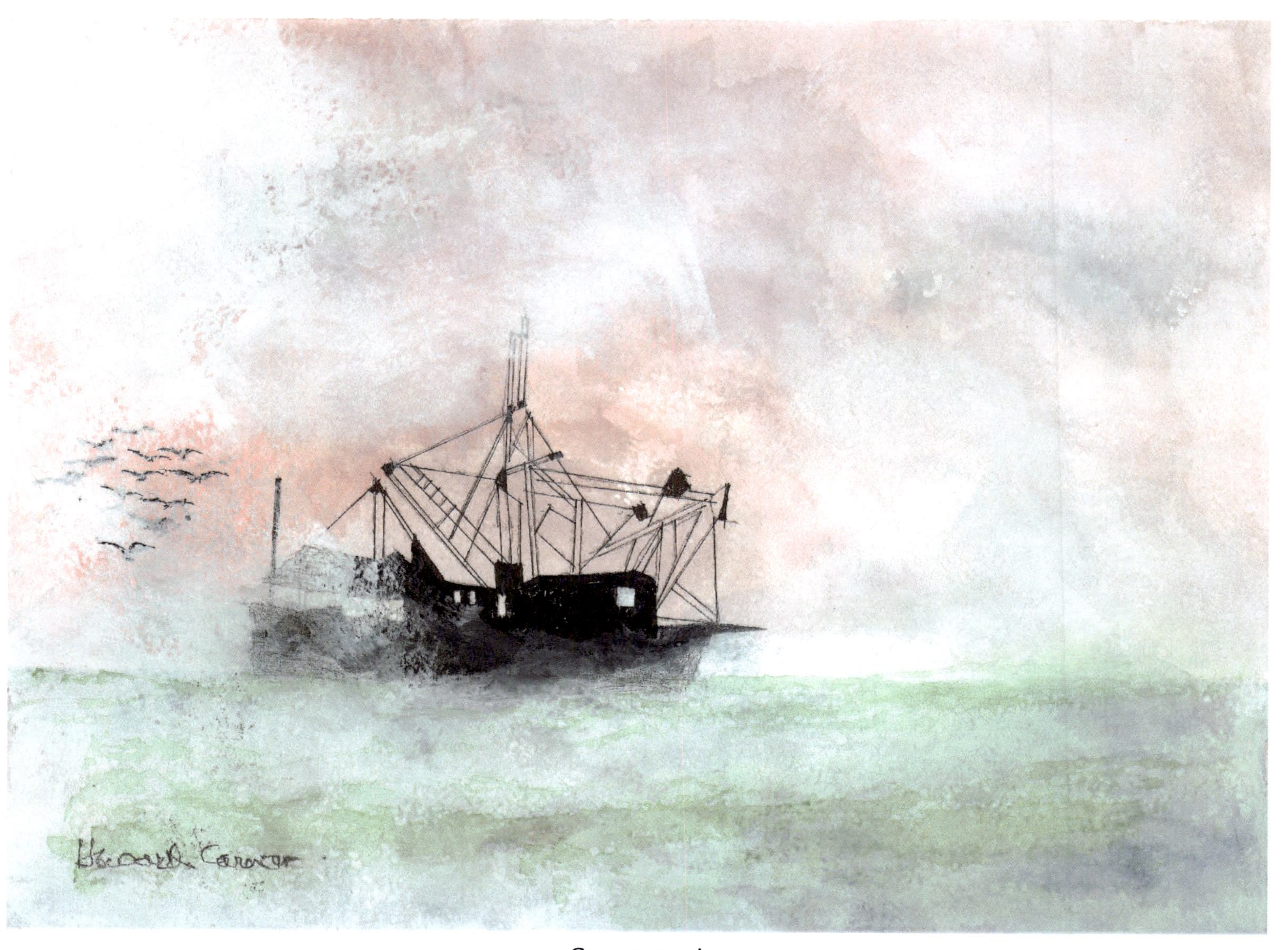

SHRIMPIN'

SABLE ISLAND DAWN

Hunter's Moon lays a magenta robe
across dawn's shoulders, then slinks
behind cumulus curtains—
down a spiral stair into the sea's cellar.

Salt-tongued northeasterlies
lick the water green. Whitecaps
shoulder sand onto the backs
of enchanted dunes, where marram
holds fast, sandwort keeps low,
sirens and selkies bewitch wild horses.

Gulls break the spell, squawking
at a ghost in the mist—
Andrea Gail, before the storm,
before the reckoning.

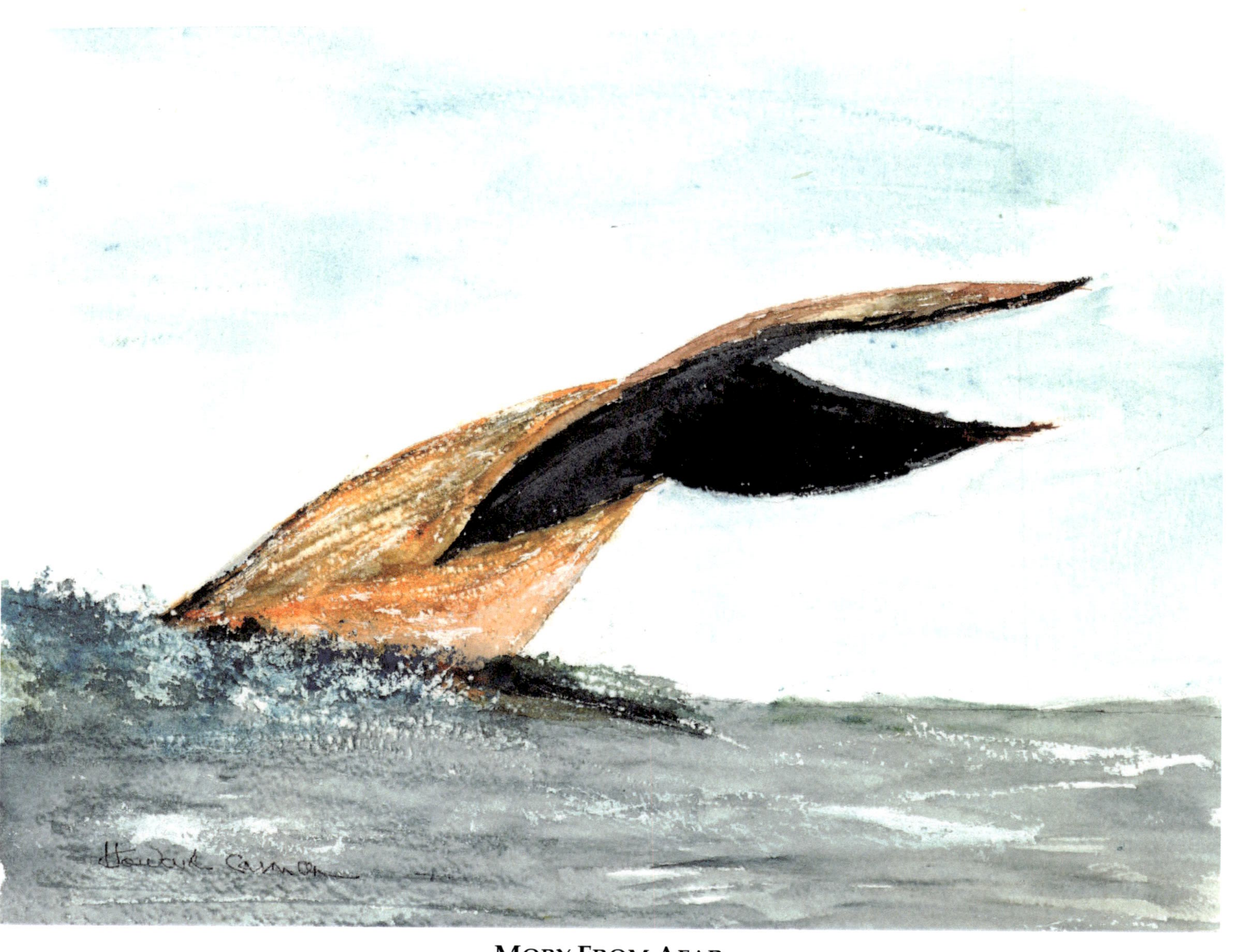

MOBY FROM AFAR

WATER DEEPER THAN DAYLIGHT

Your peace is the sea's will.
— Robert Penn Warren

Tashtego saw it first—
leviathan breaching boundary
between azure ocean and summer sky,
fluke arrogant against clouds
before sinking into seafoam.

Obsessed met obsession.
Monomania launched boats—
wood, rope, iron—soon splinters
in the sea, crew scattered
in familiar dark of moonlit Pacific.

Dawn returned—
sun like yolk in a pan—
and vengeance cast
its long shadow forward.

Fate's hemp strangled hope
and pulled it under—
to a depth neither whale
nor light has ever known.

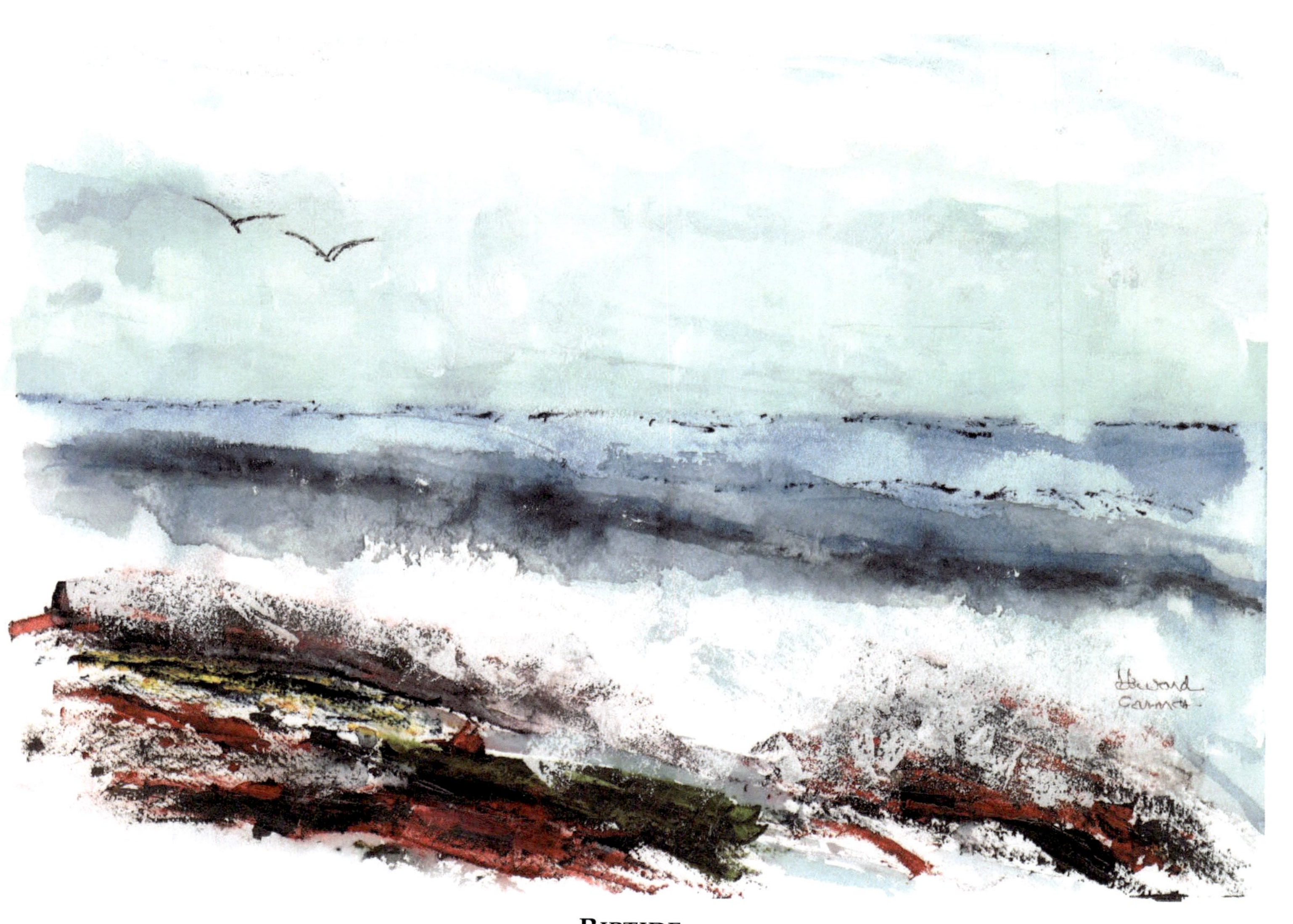

RIPTIDE

EVENTIDE

Waves from the Irish Sea
     lick our feet as we recline
          on the rocky shore
     beneath Blackhead Lighthouse.
     We share Drumshanbo gin,
one sip at a time, from a bottle
nestled upon your lap. Moonlight shivers
          on the rolling sea.
       My arm drapes
     your silky shoulder;
my hand cups your breast
as it rises and falls
     with each breath, in time
        with undulating waves.
     You—and the breeze—
     caress my hair.
The moon winks
     and says, "I want a sip."
     We smile and answer,
"Come get it."

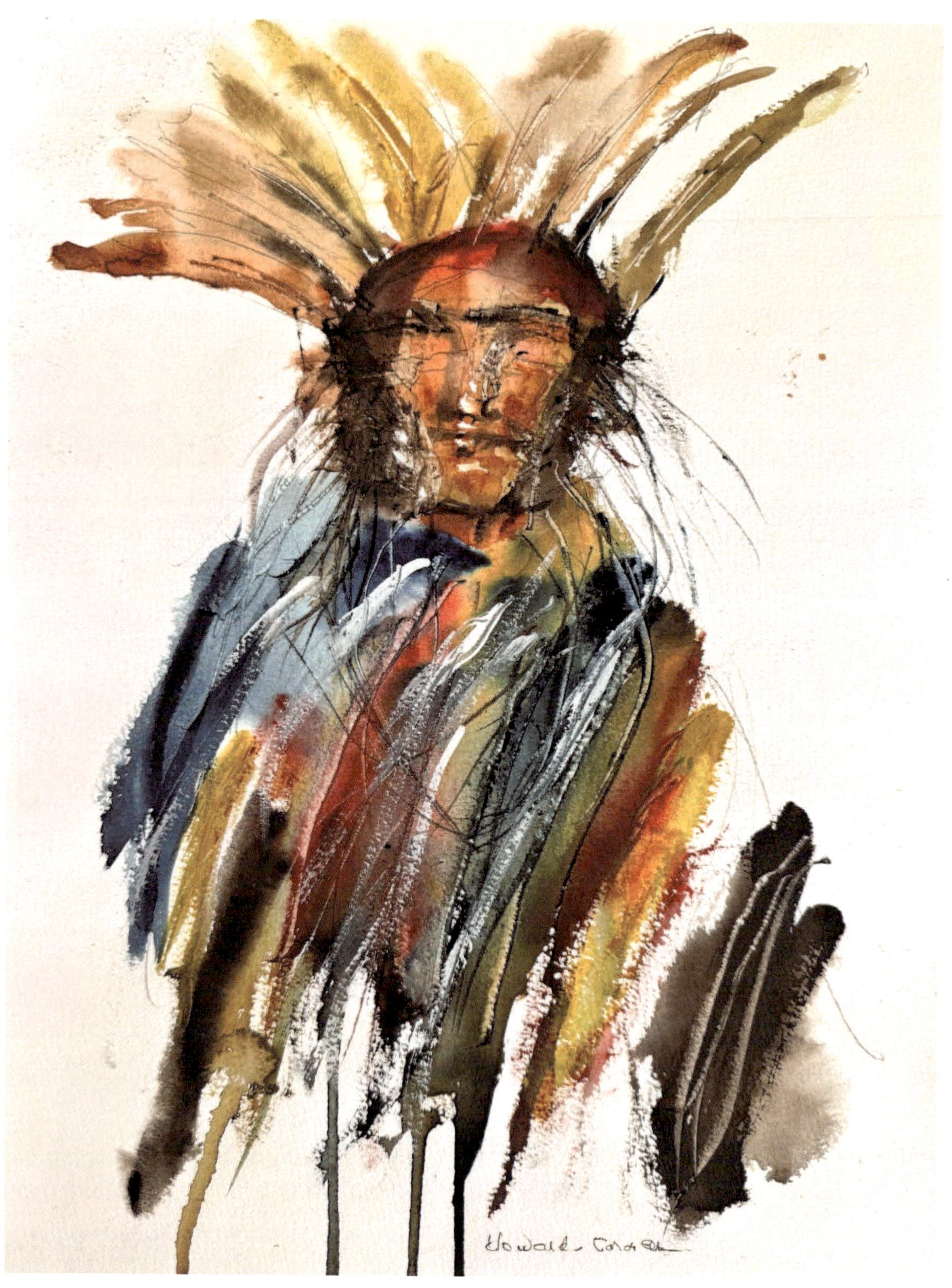

CHIEF

EX SITU CONSERVATION

for Ray Young Bear

Pedicel of Algonquin corymb,
Meskwaki people were pruned
by history and hegemony,
replanted in soil distant
from Eastern Woodlands red earth
where Wisakeha formed
and named them.

French fur traders
called them Foxes,
ravaged their tribe,
forced survivors
to find new fields.

Fifth generation cubs
preserve their past
and, with hope, dredge
fertile Iowa loam. Ancestors
filter through their fingers
beneath casino lights that eclipse
constellations they named
many futures ago.

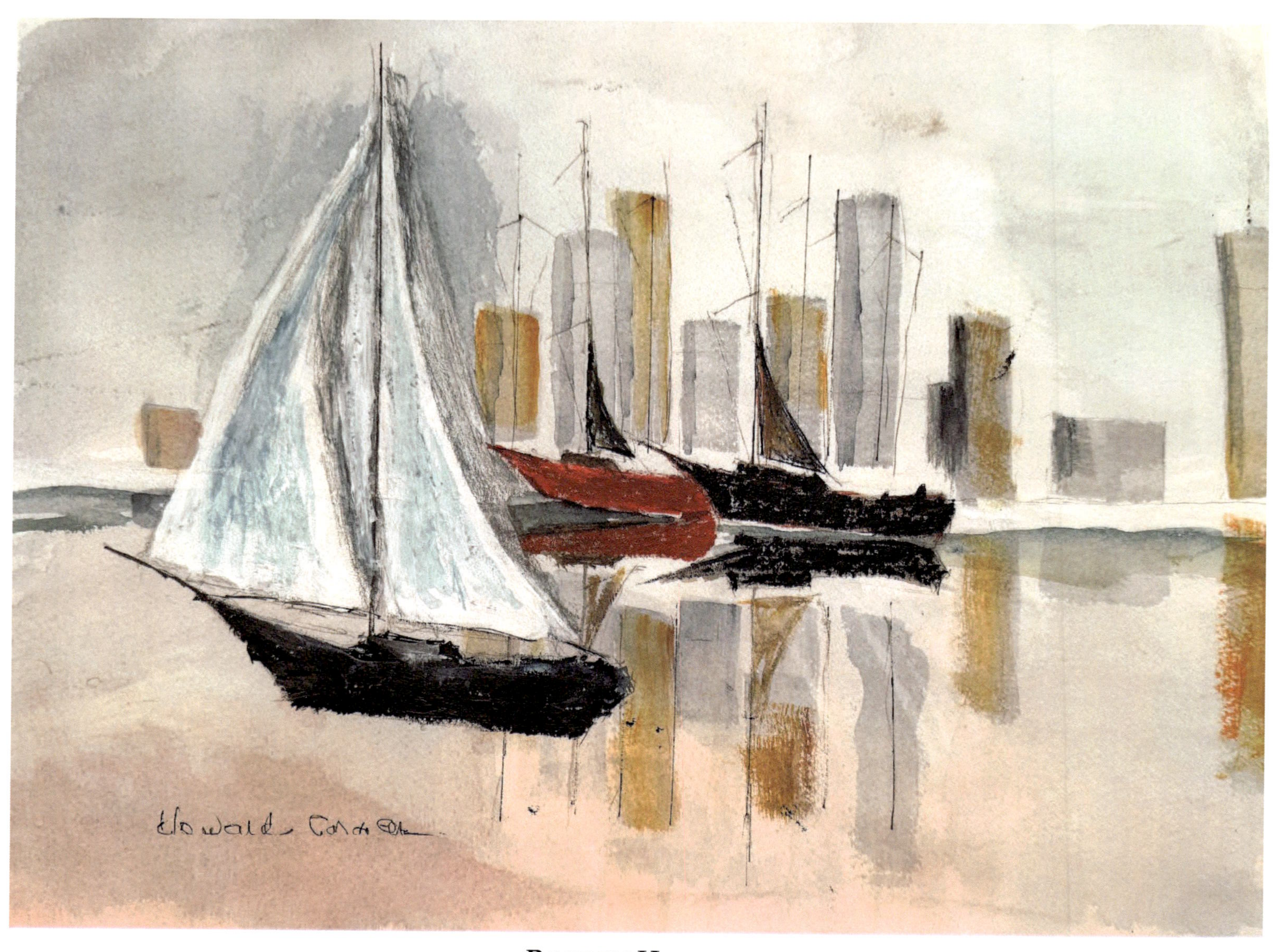

Boston Harbor

BOSTON HARBOR, 1980

for Reg, Marie, Paul, and John

Tide lower than Earth's cellar floor,
    mud breached spaces between bare toes
half mile seaward of Carson Beach.
    We crabbed for hopes with mesh baskets
and talked of dreams between breaths
    of cannabis smoke blown
through moonbeams into ocean's darkness.
    Baskets still empty at dawn,
we raced each other—and the tide—back to shore.

Unpredicted dreams fulfilled,
    we are now scattered
across geography, history, and significance,
    like shells of limpet, moonsnail, and cockle
across the Massachusetts shore.
    Futures soon past, only a poem will recall
memories sweeter than Mary Jane
    and brighter than June's full moon
over Boston Harbor.

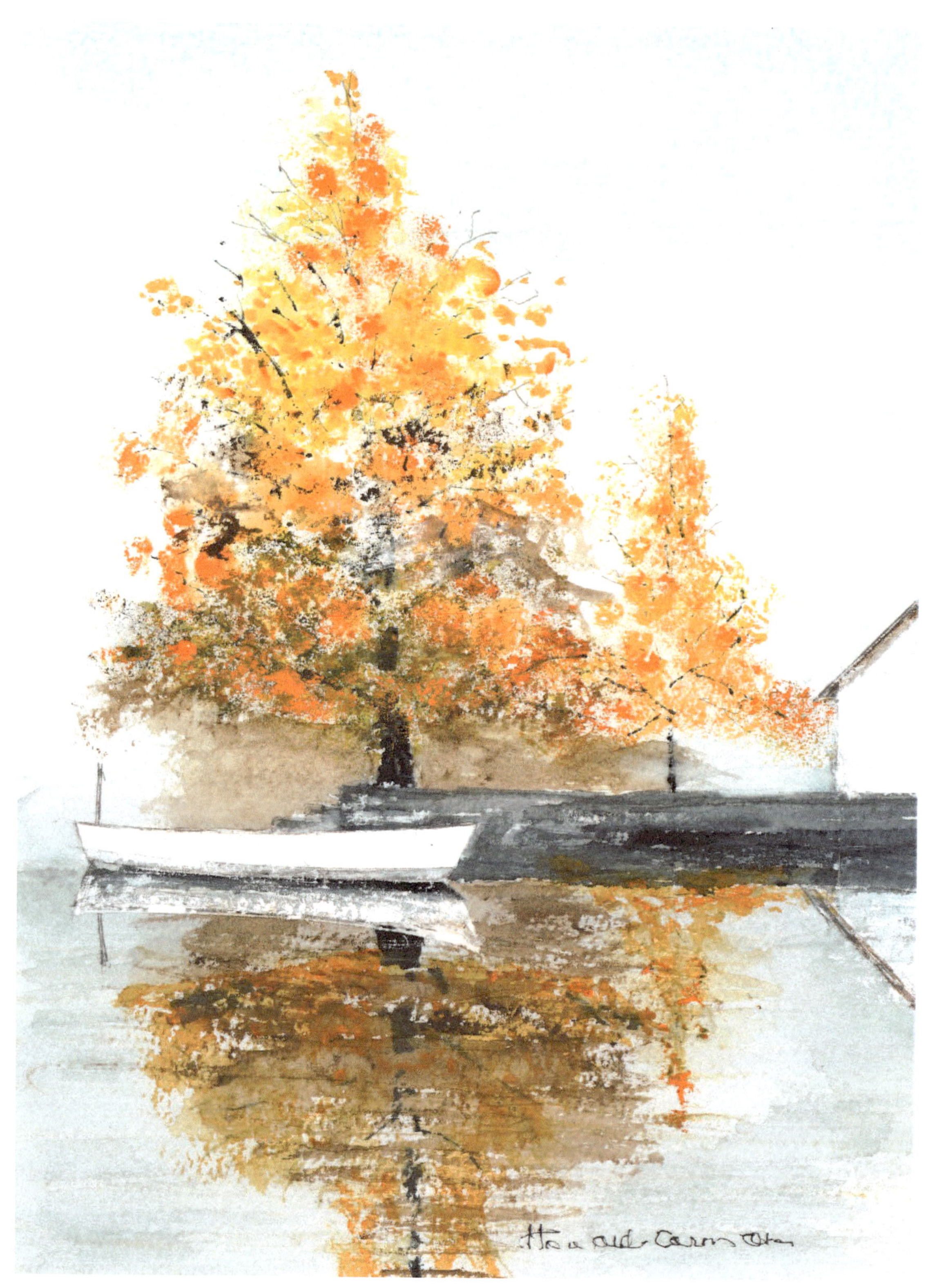

FALL REFLECTIONS

SEASONS PAST

for Ted Germroth

Autumn's chill chased
October's orange to the lakefront,
supplanted summer sweat.
We rowed together, our reflections
chasing us across wind-rippled waters
between sun-drenched shores
of nowhere and everywhere.

Now solstice: near-black too early
as darkness outruns daylight.
Shagbark hickories
and sugar maples stand leafless
beside the lake, our oars
against the wall
of your empty boathouse.

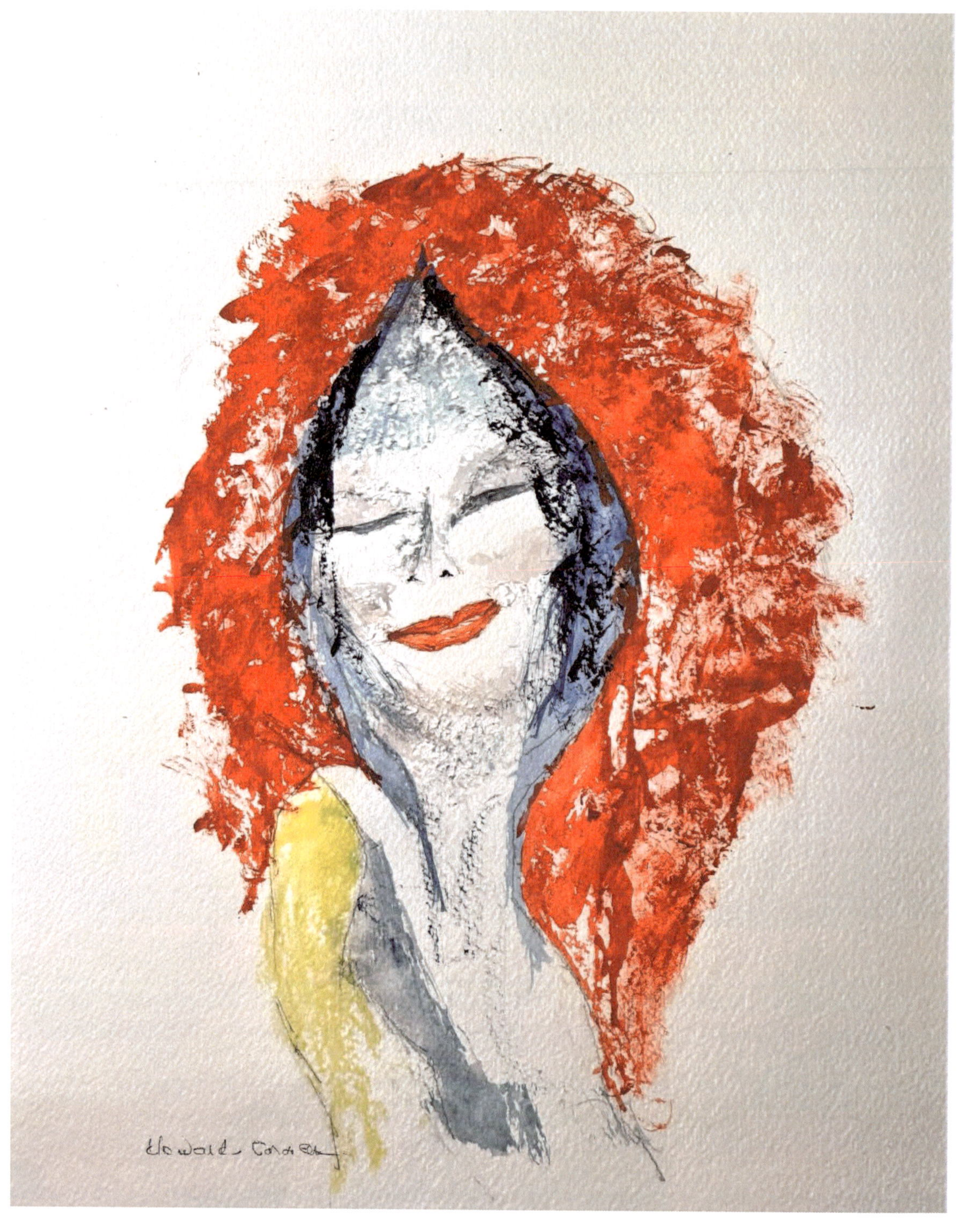

CLARA

CLARA

You took me to Figueres,
introduced me to Dalí. The day—
and my clock—began to melt.

On Montjuïc, you spread your arms—
no words, only body telling the truth.
Your hair caught the air
like a fan unfurling, like a hoopoe
in flight above Sagrada Família.

At Mercat de Santa Catarina,
we ate olives, spit pits like children,
shared the juices on our lips.

I kissed the butterfly
inked on your shoulder.
It belonged to you—
until it belonged to the past.

Surreal. Like Dalí.
Daydream, of course.
But the taste is vivid.

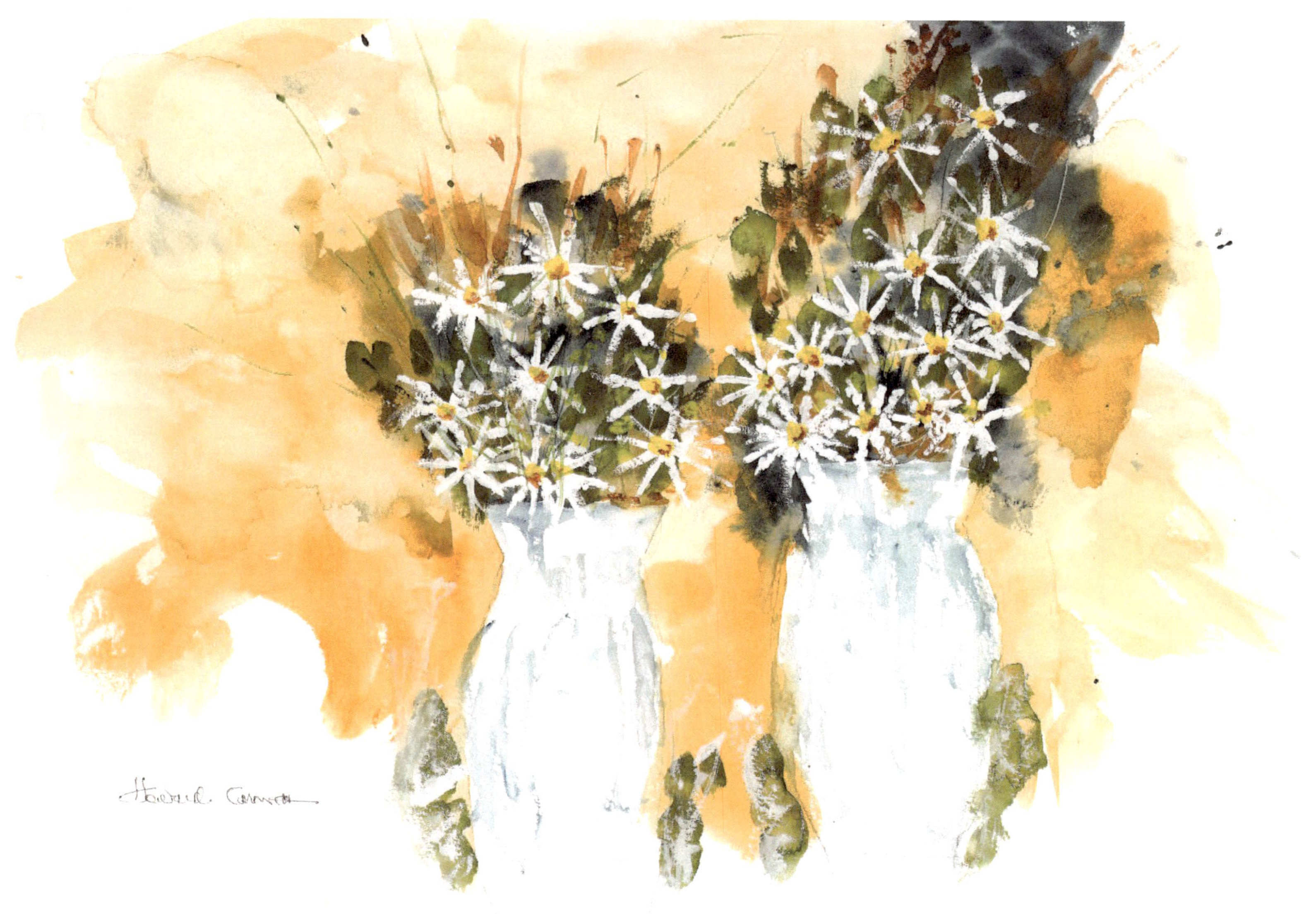

Shasta Daisies

SUNBURST

for the "Crew" on Sunburst Cove

Flower Moon sets
as morning slips
through pellucid panes,
lays quiet ochre—
a hush of light—
on dining room wall.

On a mahogany table,
blossoms from far-flung fields
mingle and settle into crystal vases,
stems supporting and leaning
upon one another,
like loving neighbors
in a suburban cul-de-sac—

holding space and filling gaps
grief has passed through.

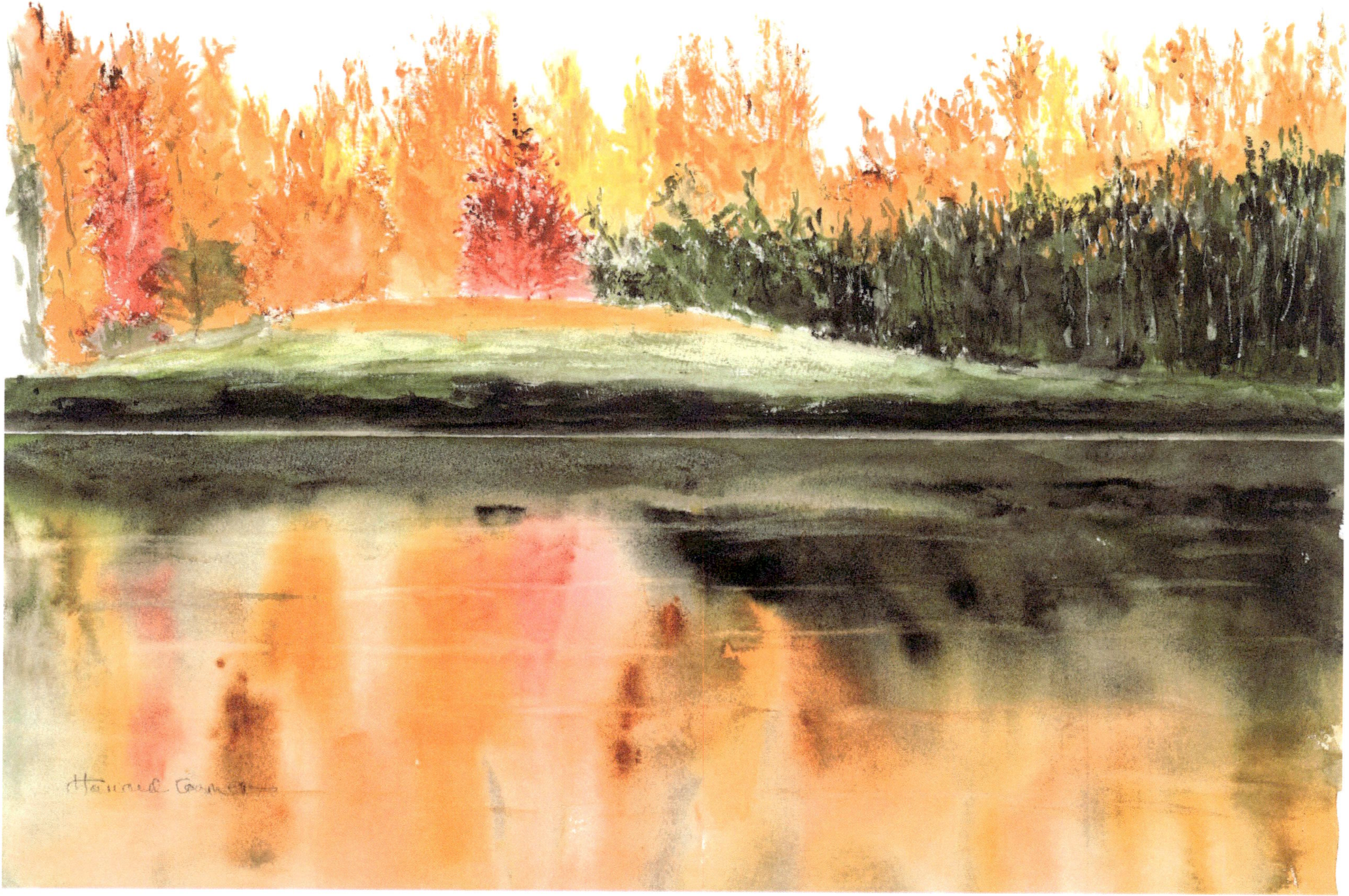

Hatchie Coon, Arkansas

GHOSTS

after KB Ballentine

We hiked this trail together
before you became an echo,
our passionate lakeside kisses
now ash, adrift in the water.

I am walking toward the pyre.
My boots hang open.
I need you to know: I am ready
to dip our toes and begin again.

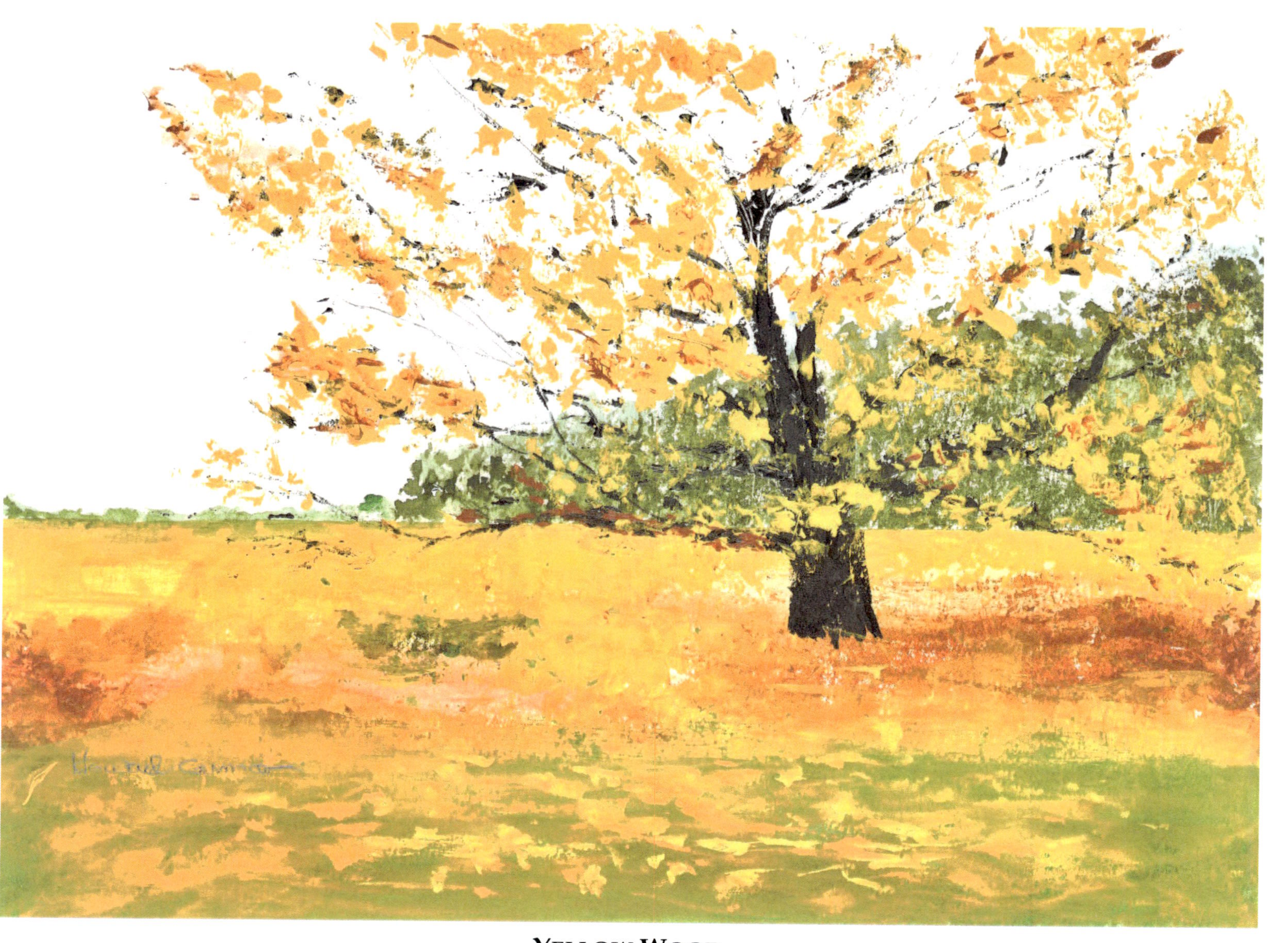

Yellow Wood

I WONDER

*So you come to poetry not out of what
you know, but out of what you wonder.*
—*Lucille Clifton*

Did W.S. Merwin and Mary Oliver ever meet,
gaze into one another's eyes, shake hands
that wielded pencils to capture their worlds
and our imaginations?

Do they enjoy each other's company now,
sit together in a celestial field of grass,
watch *Spring Azures*, savor *The View*,
admire *Shore Birds* while they survey *The Sea?*

Do they remember the *anniversary of his death*,
walk together through her *cottage of darkness*,
and greet Emerson, who has come
to *turn the key and bolt the door?*

Maybe they sip coffee with Jesus and the Buddha,
revel in newfound discoveries, find answers
to questions they provoked us all to ponder—
what is and who has a soul?

Perhaps they stroll quietly through the woods,
listen closely for the *echo of the future*,
and wonder, as I do:
what if Frost had taken the other road?

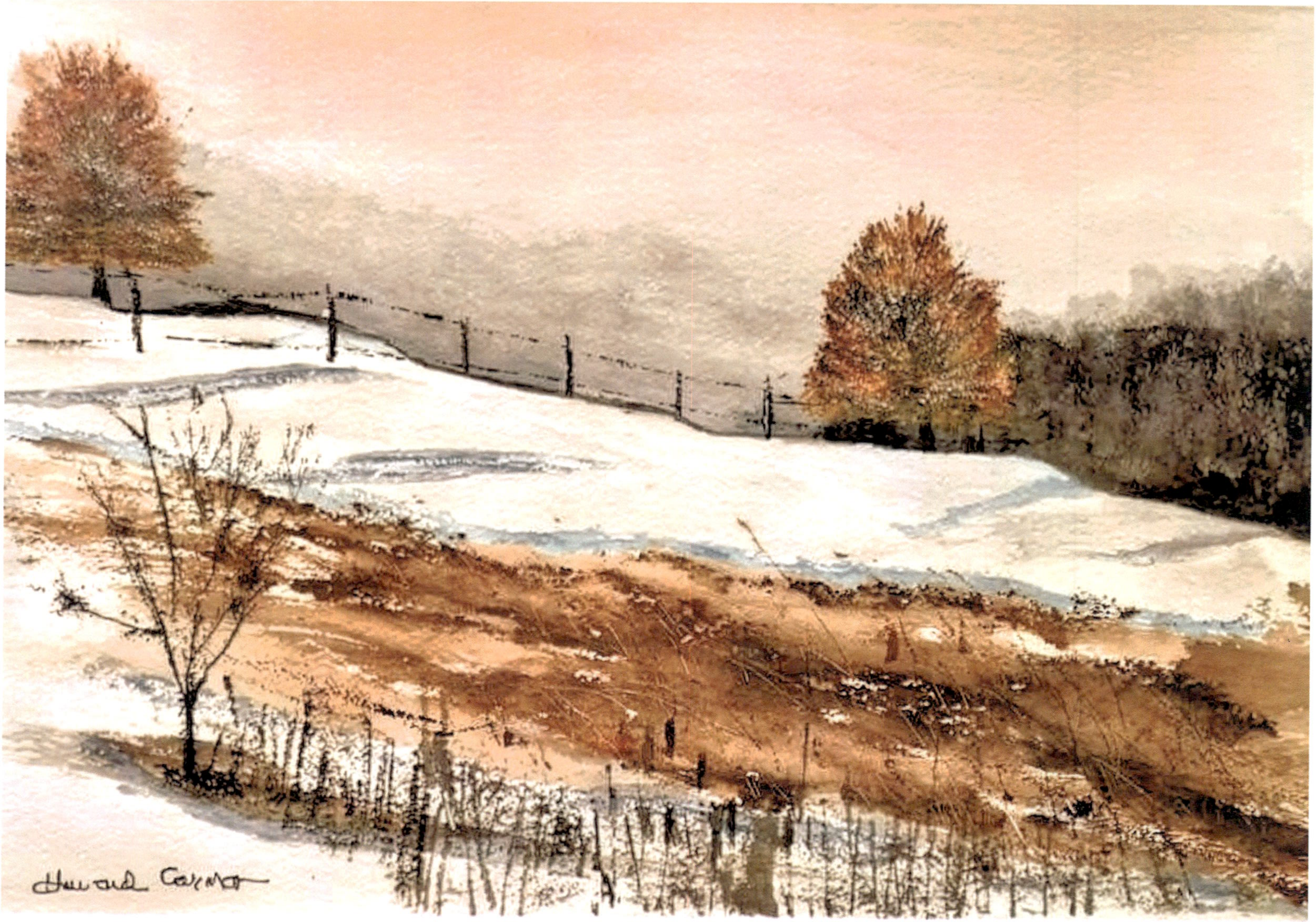

Approaching Winter

OBION COUNTY, TENNESSEE

Gloaming brushes sepia
through brambles and briars.
Past a fault scarp, white oak rails
ride red cedar posts, where lowing cattle
graze fescue and orchardgrass.

Chips and *yips* bounce
from loess hills as cardinals
and coyotes play hide-and-seek
in sassafras, sugarberry,
and dim creek bottoms.

Here, above the clouds, Aba' Binni'Li'
blued Chickasaw skies, yellowed holy fires,
listened for turtle shell rattles
and stomp dance thunder.

Upon this hallowed loam, our people
planted soybeans and corn—
and family trees.
Built homesteads and businesses.
Bequeathed gravestones and memories.

And, now, paintings and poems.

ACKNOWLEDGMENTS

Senior:

Many thanks to Fred Rawlinson and wife, Jo. For 12 years, Fred, a marvelous painter, took on the task of teaching me to paint. He taught me and became my mentor. He and Jo encouraged me every step along the way. Anna Parker, a fellow student of Fred's, whose work in the style of pointillism is remarkable, has often lifted my spirit—and my brush. Millie Brummet, dear friend whose work in oil is incredible, has always challenged me and encouraged me to excel to the next level. And many thanks to the staff at Memphis Professional Imaging for scanning and digitizing the paintings: Cliff Satterfield, Cynthia Poole, Emilee Pittman, and Buck Billings consistently do amazing work. Most of all, thank you, Junior. Who would have thought that engineer father and chemist son would take up painting and poetry upon retirement and publish a book together? Not me, but I am so happy we did. Thanks for the journey—and the memories.

Junior:

I want to thank countless friends, mentors, and fellow poets who have encouraged, challenged, critiqued, and taught. Hopefully you know who you are … you are far too many to name here. Special thanks to Will Wright, developmental editor and wonderful friend, who has patiently guided me and walked with me down the path to becoming a better poet. To my high school English teacher, Brother Joel McGraw, who planted a seed I failed to water for way too long. To Rose and Janice, who graciously welcomed me to Poetry Society of Tennessee (PST). To Lisa—poet, visionary, and PST president—who righted the ship and let me help steer it. To my critique group partners: Lisa, Harvey, Fred, Margaret, Kayla, Sarah, Molly, Lydia, Liam. To workshop leaders and contest sponsors and judges. To those who have encouraged me every step of the way . . . Connie, Pat, KB, Danita, John, Jesse, Jake, Cyd, Russell, Shuly . . . the list goes on. To Karen, who travels the journey with me and always provides a soft place to land when the muse drops me and disappears. Most of all, thank you, Pops, without whom none of this (poetry nor life) would have happened.

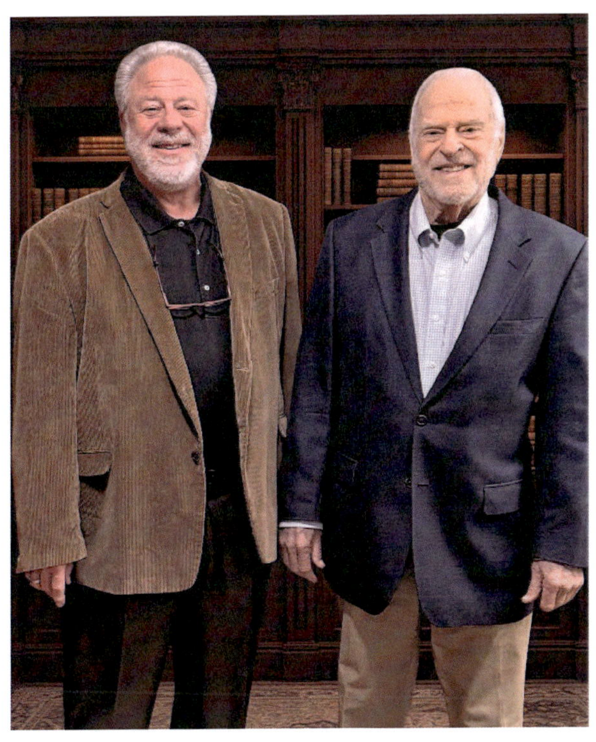

ABOUT THE AUTHORS

Howard S. Carman, Sr. ("Pops") retired in 2010 (age 73) after a career that began at age 17 drafting house plans in his hometown of Union City, TN. It ended more than 50 years later in higher education administration (capital project management) at The University of Tennessee Health Science Center (Memphis). Roles along the way included apprentice carpenter, draftsman, and professional engineer (structural), showing little interest in art or painting. Early in his career, he befriended well-known watercolor artist Fred Rawlinson, who occupied an office in the same campus building. For retirement, Pops' wife, Beverly, gave him tuition for Fred's class, "Introduction to Watercolor Painting." He has continued painting since.

Howard S. Carman, Jr., Ph.D. ("Junior") retired in 2018 (age 59) after a 32-year career as an R&D chemist. A swellheaded scientist, he disdained literature, especially poetry, during his educational and career years. That changed during a spirituality retreat in 2011, when he wrote the first poem he ever kept. He has continued writing since. He published his first collection (*But Now I See: Rhymes and Reflections*) in 2017. Upon retirement, he joined Poetry Society of Tennessee and serves on its Board of Directors. Recent poetry appears in *Tennessee Voices Anthology, Black Moon Magazine,*

Abyss & Apex, Braided Way Magazine, Troublesome Rising Digital Anthology, and *A Place for All Voices* anthology.

Poems Previously Published:

"Homestead" in *But Now I See: Rhymes and Reflections* (2017)

"Marvel at the Sunrise" (slightly revised) as "Dance Over My Dust" in *Tennessee Voices Anthology, 2023-2024.*

"Remembering Tomorrows" (slightly revised) in *Tennessee Voices Anthology, 2023-2024.*

"Mann Gulch, 1949" (slightly revised) in *Tennessee Voices Anthology, 2021-2022. Originally written in response to the photograph "No Escape" by Lisa Kamolnick. See https://lisakamolnick.com/tag/pst/*

T.S. Eliot quote from "Four Quartets" by T.S. Eliot, with permission from Faber and Faber Ltd.